T0088934

FROM **CONVICTION** to **REDEMPTION**

A Memoir as told to Danielle N. Andrews

STEPHEN BOBO AND DANIELLE ANDREWS

This book is a work of non-fiction. Unless otherwise noted, the author and the publisher make no explicit guarantees as to the accuracy of the information contained in this book and in some cases, names of people and places have been altered to protect their privacy.

Balboa Press books may be ordered through booksellers or by contacting:

Balboa Press
A Division of Hay House
1663 Liberty Drive
Bloomington, IN 47403
www.balboapress.com
844-682-1282

Because of the dynamic nature of the Internet, any web addresses or links contained in this book may have changed since publication and may no longer be valid. The views expressed in this work are solely those of the author and do not necessarily reflect the views of the publisher, and the publisher hereby disclaims any responsibility for them.

The author of this book does not dispense medical advice or prescribe the use of any technique as a form of treatment for physical, emotional, or medical problems without the advice of a physician, either directly or indirectly. The intent of the author is only to offer information of a general nature to help you in your quest for emotional and spiritual well-being. In the event you use any of the information in this book for yourself, which is your constitutional right, the author and the publisher assume no responsibility for your actions.

Print information available on the last page.

ISBN: 978-1-9822-6114-6 (sc)
ISBN: 978-1-9822-6115-3 (e)

Balboa Press rev. date: 01/13/2021

CONTENTS

FOREWORD

They say hindsight is 20/20, and as I sat down to write this book with an erroneous thought that I had my life figured out by now, the process of remembering and chronicling my experiences humbled me. Coming to the realization that no matter what graces and mercies God gave me, I was determined to do things as I saw fit. There was a time in my life when nothing or none could tell me anything. I always knew best, even when I didn't. Pride was my friend and guide.

Thinking that way almost ended me several times over. His voice (God's) and his silence tried to guide me to a more righteous life and my rejection and running from him only added to my perilous journey that I had to travel. No one bought this ticket for this crazy ride, but me. I bought it and stamped it myself.

The things I have been through both good and bad have proven that God is a true father protecting when necessary and correcting when needed. My butt has been whooped, I've been put in time out, and straight told to sit my ass down! He has also given precious gifts, sound advice and unconditional love through it all. People were placed in my path to teach me, guide me, warn me, and love me. Not all of these people I recognized right away, and some I had to lose before I knew how precious they really were.

My story will contain some uncomfortable situations, shocking confessions, Ungodly language at times, but this is my authentic life. Good Bad Ugly or Indifferent, it's my journey. One that is far from finished. The old folks used to say that God protects children and fools. Well, I certainly wasn't a child!

Know that this is not a self-help book. I'm not claiming to be able to change anyone's life. I'm just a guy who has witnessed and lived through some things that should have killed me several times over. I am a regular man who made terrible choices and God still saw fit to bring me pockets of joy that I was too caught up in my pride to see. They say that "If you can't be a good example, be a terrible warning." Hopefully, I can be both. I can be an example of "an old dog learning a few new tricks" and warning to not wait until rock bottom finds you.

My hope for you, the reader, will find comfort, inspiration, and maybe even a few laughs from my journey from football, to Pro wrestling, to my life on both sides of the bars and everywhere in between.

Humble Thanks and God Bless,
Bo.

To Mom:

I don't need to rehash all the trials and tribulations that we've been through. However, no matter what went wrong or right; I knew you would always be there. I cannot put a price on how valuable your presence in my life is. Whether it was on the rainy/ snowy sidelines of weekend Peewee Football games, while sitting in that uncomfortable ass chair in the emergency room when I broke a bone, standing over me while I did homework before I even thought about going out, sitting in in the crowd – cheering me on while I threw grown men around a ring and took hits to the face and chest, and making sure I ate while you went without. Even at the worst, when you found out I was going to jail, your love never failed me. Even as I write this, I know you are bragging to somebody about "your baby".

Thank you for the tough love, the fun love, long distance love, and never ending real OG love. You are amazing and did everything to ensure I would be too.

Words cannot even express my gratitude.

With All My Love,
Stephen

dna

CHAPTER 1

Hindsight is 20/20

As I sat on a bus heading to CRC, watching Dayton get smaller and smaller, I was struck with an overwhelming need to know what the fuck was happening to my life. I also found myself wandering down memory lane. Thinking of my Momma and what she must be thinking of me right now. God knows I wasn't born an inmate. (None of us are.) I just knew that that night in April, 1971; my mother holding her brand new 13-pound baby in The Ohio State Hospital, never thought in a million years that he would end up sitting on a modified school bus heading for the most unwanted education he could imagine. Where was my father? I haven't the foggiest, as he had been a phantom, blowing in and out of my life since my failed football career. I can't help but wonder, in hindsight, if his sporadic presence (or lack thereof) was what led to my sitting in shackles on a hard ass bus seat frightened and pissed off royally.

I'm very proud of my heritage, I'm half Samoan. However, I missed out on learning more about my father's side of the family. My parent's relationship fell apart and I didn't really see much of him until I'd started to mature and show promise on the football field, a common interest we held. My father played football in college and was signed to play for the Chicago Bears. Of course, he would wish his son to go pro. The question still remained a thorn in my side as to why I wasn't good enough to stick around and raise? Was it that his own pursuits were more important than raising his little boy? However, when the possibility of the family business being passed to another generation became a possibility, POOF, insta-daddy is born. I would be a liar if I said some part of me wasn't happy to have him even though we both knew it wasn't out of any kind of reparations or longing to be a part of my life, but there was a deep rage that sat in the pit of my stomach wanting to scream and cry and cuss the soul out of this fair weather father. Love is complicated. It has you angry and longing for someone at the same time. This wouldn't be the last time my thoughts would come to settle on a complicated father/ son relationship.

Mom chose to raise me as a single mother. She had the loving support of my grandparents. I was raised in my mother's hometown, Springfield Ohio. My life as the only child was wonderful. I never wanted for anything. I had the male influence of my grandfather and two beautiful strong women to show me the type of woman I needed in my life. I can't say I didn't miss having a dad around for the stereotypical fatherly moments. But, hey, what can you do? You can't make someone want to be a part of your life. I had Momma, and Grandma and Grandpaw and that was a winning combination no matter how you slice it. Mom and Grandma were "no nonsense"; they expected great things from me and anything less would incur the wrath. As I am of a certain age, I came from an era when Grandma would jack you up as bad as Momma when you messed up. I remember a time when I was roughly 10 years old and was out playing with neighborhood friends. They belonged to the Boy Scouts and it was time for them to leave for their meeting some 4 blocks away at a church. I asked my mother if I could join them. She replied, "No, it's almost dinner time." Usually, this would have been a sufficient answer and I would have sadly said goodbye and went inside. Not today. Instead I decided to go anyway and Mom would be fine. So, here I was hanging out with the Boy Scouts and meeting and greeting…then Momma came in. Cue the scary music here. Mom had a fire in her eyes that told me that it was a good thing that I was sitting in that church. She looked at me in the eye and said, "So, you just gonna decide to go where you want anyway?" When I tell you that my mind was racing for an answer that may save my life, or at least my behind, I mean it! The best thing I could come up with was, "I thought I could go and be back before dinner?" Her look never changed and I knew she was not impressed with this impromptu explanation. Needless to say, I got my tail end worn out! Then getting home, Grandma got me again! I literally could not sit down. I stood there at the table, not daring to sit my 'heated seat' on anything hard. To add insult to injury, dinner was hamburgers and French fries! I love burgers and fries! However, there was no burger for me. I was Chef Boyardee ravioli. No contest to Momma's burgers. I must've not have learned my lesson, because I had the nerve to complain! To which, Grandpaw shut it down with, "There's hamburger in the ravioli". Damn. This wasn't the only time this dynamic duo snatched me in line. It just goes to show that I had a strong foundation of discipline growing up. So how did I end up heading to prison? I just couldn't wrap my head around it.

As I mentioned before, I didn't hear from Dad much until I started to show promise in football. It's safe to say that, besides my Momma, football was my first love. I have always loved the game of football. As a kid, I could always be found either watching football or playing football. Of course, as an eighties kid, I had G.I Joe, Transformers and the like. However, Football was my first love, well besides my Momma. I can recall being about 7 years old, and being in the hospital with my mother and grandmother visiting my grandfather, who was recovering from complications due to diabetes. As anyone with kids knows, or at least, if you remember being a kid, you know how boring it was while the big people made you behave while they visited. I was in the hallway entertaining myself playing football. All the positions, touchdowns, field goals, pass rushes, it was all me. At least in my world, that's what was happening. Apparently, I was entertaining someone else as well. An older gentleman was watching me as I played, and I suppose he saw talent in what I was doing. I also was bigger than the average bear and would be quite the asset to a peewee team. He approached my mom and suggested that I try out for the local peewee team. She didn't even NEED to ask me if I was interested! Sign me up, NOW! I get to play football for real. Suited up like my heroes on Sundays. Just like that, I was bit by the football bug. I played football through my elementary years, junior high school and High school. Somewhere in these years, Mom and I had moved to Dayton, Ohio. I attended Meadowdale High School. I was proud to be a Meadowdale Lion. It was here that I was given the moniker, Bozilla. I was 15, well over 6 feet tall and about 300 pounds. I had some serious moves and was merciless on the field. If you were in my way, you were getting mowed down. That was my job, and I did it well. Like most young men, I had dreams of going pro. The way it was going for me on the field it was a great possibility. One I was willing to work for. My mother was a teacher and very intelligent. She loved that her son was a great football player, but she also made sure I was a respectful young man. Above all, no son of Annette (now Woods) was going to be a dummy. She and my stepdad wouldn't hesitate to shut the football train down if my grades weren't up to par. However, Mom was up against a bigger adversary than my dislike of math. There was a system that valued my talent on the field and my prospect of putting their school on the map more than my academic development. Even if I did struggle in a subject, I never really had to suffer for my lack of performance. I was passed along, given less challenging classes to insure my passing and praised for mediocre work. Not until recently, did I recognize that this pattern of underachievement would fuel a mindset; and it fuels many a mindset in students around the country. It also fuels a term that is just getting recognition, the School to Prison Pipeline. Briefly, it is a system that basically paves the way for children to end up as juveniles and maybe even later, adults in the penal system. This will be discussed later towards the end.

I mentioned my stepfather. His name was Harold Woods My mother married him in 1985. To say I was happy for them would be completely incorrect. I didn't care for him at all. He was a man that was determined to parent my childish ways out of me. I resented him for that. I'd been the only child my whole life, and let's be honest, I was spoiled. Harold didn't want me to be another entitled kid running the streets. My mindset was, I'd gotten along this far without a father, what was he here for? Besides that I was 14 years old, and anyone out there with children knows that 14 year olds are moody, and prone to be resentful when everything is ideal. I'm sure Harold knew what was up when he married my mom and I'm positive, that I didn't make it easy. Harold tried to instill a sense of responsibility, hard work, and respect in me. I wasn't disrespectful child. He would tell me to depend on myself. Not to look for people to rescue me. To take care of my family and to work hard and smart simultaneously. He insisted that I do my best and be my best at all times. He demanded nothing but my best from me. Why did I resent someone who only wished for me to be a stand up man? Because it meant growing and being uncomfortable at times. Our relationship was contentious at times. When my mother had a stroke and a brain hemorrhage, and almost left me forever, Harold, in his pain and fear of losing her, blamed me for her illness. I was a 16 year old kid, to whom his mother was his whole world to be face to face with her demise, and hen to be told it was my fault, was devastating. Our already strained relationship became more strained. How could he blame me? However, as a kid, I still considered the possibility that maybe I did do something to stress her out to this point. I prayed that God would fix my mom. I always knew about God, but was never very religious. I prayed because I was expected to. Because Grandma taught me to. I knew all the Hail Marys and Lord's Prayers. (Grandma was Catholic). How would I survive without her? It was the two of us against the world! I certainly couldn't depend on my father and Harold wasn't exactly embracing me. I was truly lost. Momma had to see me go to my first prom from her hospital bed. A fact that Harold made me feel bad about again. "How can you go and enjoy your prom when your mother is lying here dying?" I realize now, that his words came from fear and worry, but as a child, those words cut deeply.

God has a way of working things out at their darkest and Thank God, Momma recovered and came home to further heal. I was so grateful to have more time with my mother. God had spoken to me by threatening my safety net, but just like Momma's warning about going with my friends, I didn't listen. As a matter of fact, my life was about to take a turn that would change me forever. The events around her illness had cast a dark shadow over me. I was left with some emotions that I didn't know how to deal with. Around this time, I started to dabble in selling and running drugs. I see it now as my misguided way to deal with feeling out of control and aggressive. I mean, who were the baddest boys on the block? Feared or respected, the dope dealers had a place in my society. I could deal with my control issues because who was gonna mess with me? I could also make (what I saw as) good money. Momma wouldn't have to work so hard to help me. I was told that her working so hard is what led to stroke and aneurysm. She would never have to worry about me again, or so I thought. Harold would get off my back because I was "working" maybe even I could gain some type of respect from him.

I was still in high school and playing my role as the jock. I was a talented football player in school and I'd certainly caught a few eyes of people while on the field. One set of eyes I never expected to show up was my father. After years of not really having any contact with him what so ever, he shows up. Wanting to be a part of my life. The job of raising me was about over and now you want to show an interest?! Where were you when I was playing peewee in the rain and cold weather? Where were you when my mom was out there running up and down the sidelines- alone? When it was parent's night and my teammates had both parents (whether still together or not) on either side of them, why was my left side exposed? It was mom who signed those permission slips to let me play. Now I'm a junior in High school and whispers of college ball and even going pro are swirling, and like a shark smelling blood in the water, you appear? For what? I wouldn't let my father too close to me during this time, as I really didn't trust his motives. Oh, we talked but it wasn't like a Hallmark movie for sure. I couldn't tell if he wanted to guide me, or juice me. I always had the questions, but never the guts to ask. In my quiet moments and my low moments, like now, sitting on a prison bus running through my life, trying to sort it out, what was so hard about wishing me a happy birthday (if you ever remembered it), sending a Christmas card, or coming to see me play BEFORE I was a big deal? I loved Grady L. Bobo in my own way. I just wished I'd asked what happened to make him fall so far back for so long. He has since passed. Some things I guess will not be revealed until we meet again.

CHAPTER 2

The Best Laid Plans

While staring out the window of the bus, listening to the sound of the shackles clanking against the metal walls and floor of the bus, I aw a car go by with California plates. I can't even tell you the type of car it was, but it got me reminiscing again about finishing high school and moving clear across the country. I went to Berkley College in California. My football skills had gotten me there on scholarship. I was fortunate to play first string as a freshman. The opportunity wasn't wasted on me. I worked hard, my goal was to go pro. As angry as I was with my father, being a pro football player like him wouldn't be such a terrible thing. Besides, I could take care of my Momma and Grandma the way they took care of me. I have to admit; it was hard being away from home. No matter what a kid says about being ready to leave home, the homesickness seeps in. I was away from my girlfriend, my friends, my whole support system was literally across the country. My days consisted of workouts, classes and practices. Of course, I went to the odd frat party, and even considered joining a fraternity myself. I won't mention names but I really wanted to act out to "Atomic Dog" by George Clinton. I wasn't sad about being so far away from home, but I was certainly feeling on my own. As with all life changes, the feeling of fear was certainly mixed with excitement. My major in school was law enforcement. I mean, I'd always prided myself on being a protector and I always looked out for those who couldn't protect themselves. Although I was studying to be a police officer (yeah strange for a kid who was just selling weed a semester ago), my future focus was certainly on playing pro ball. I'd never really given much thought on being anything else. My dream since childhood, and my efforts since junior high had always been to play for the NFL. However, a plan B was always a good thing I was told.

Little did I know that one Saturday, in front of thousands, my aspirations to play pro would be dashed. As so many players before me, I suffered a season ending knee injury. Further examinations, said it was likely career ending. Seriously?! I was just getting the hang of this college thing. Life was finally looking somewhat like I knew what I was doing. One play, and it's over? Riding off the field on that golf cart was nauseating. How would I finish school? Berkley offered to allow me to finish my education with them, but only if I would take out loans to pay tuition. I was devastated. God? What am I to do now? He answered, "Do you hear me? Are you listening? Lean on me". Of course, I dismissed this conversation God was trying to have with me. I was freaking out about football. All I could think of I was not interested in clinging to anyone or anything but my (now defunct) football career. All I could think of was I couldn't do that to my mother, who was already still fighting to recover from an illness that I was led to believe was my fault. I was determined never to be a burden on my Momma again. Reluctantly, I packed my belongings and headed back home to the Gem City. Another reason I was ready to come back to Dayton was that the house I stayed in with the other athletes was down the street from the Crips. Yes, THOSE Crips. While I was in high school, I thought I was bad. My friends and I thought we were NWA (Niggas With Attitudes- a rap group). When I got to Cali, I realized I had no attitude, I wasn't even peeved. Those dudes down the street were the real NWA!! I needed to get back home. Besides that, I'm half Samoan. There was no SWA! (Joke)

I moved back in with my Mother. Mom and Harold had divorced by now. I'm not clear as to why they broke up, but she seemed happier, and that's what mattered to me most. It was me and Momma against the world again. I had no choice but to get some kind of college education now, so I enrolled at Sinclair Community College. My major while there was Criminal Justice. My career goals had shifted from being a police officer to working in the field of corrections because I knew, at my size, passing the exam for the police academy would be prohibitive. I still needed a job to help my mom out, so I began working loss prevention at a local grocery store, catching shoplifters. A job that got me shot on one occasion. The lesson there, sometimes, getting away with $20.00 worth of food is sometimes worth taking someone's life for, I guess. The incident, however, never, deterred me from going back to work, or wanting to continue the field of study.

Even though I had a basic grasp of what I was doing, I was still mourning the loss of my football dreams. I was no longer a jock and the benefits of sliding through classes had expired. So, I struggled getting a handle on my classes and managing my time. I was 20 and had a very elementary grasp of Algebra. I was always pretty good at History, English, Government and the like, but my study habits for anything were terrible. I spent, probably more time than I should have, in the school's student union lounge playing pool, cards, and D&D with friends. I was struggling to find purpose. I fortunately met some great people during this time, one of which was a short and spunky young lady named Danielle who was dating a buddy of mine named Bill. I had no idea that this chance meeting would lead to one of my greatest friendships. I remember her asking me and Bill one day, "Do you guys ever go to class?" You know, we never did answer her. Twenty-Seven years later, Dani, no we didn't.

So, to recap, a bum knee sent me home where I had to rethink my career path. Time to settle down and get conventional; follow plan B, right? Um, no. I decided I would pursue another great interest of mine, pro wrestling. As a kid, I watched the greats. Hulk Hogan, Andre' the Giant, Captain Lou Albano, Superfly Snuka, just to name a few. I was a huge fan and I've always been bigger than the average bear, I thought I would be a great fit. I was still pretty agile from playing football earlier, and my size didn't change. I knew it was going to be a long road from Dayton Ohio to WrestleMania, but you have to start somewhere, right? As I stated, my love for wrestling goes way back to being a kid in the eighties watching these legends on my Grandmother's television. The drama and action was awesome! These men were so powerful and agile, jumping from the top rope, with all sorts of acrobatics and antics! The action out of the ring was just as riveting! Drama and storylines every week kept me coming back for more! I guess I'd always entertained the fantasy of being in the ring. So, after I was sent home after basically being told that my football career was over, I really started to give this career path serious thought. One might ask, "How the heck would you go from the bodily demands of football to the injuries of wrestling?!" Well, the short answer to that is, you have got to be a little special.

I didn't have to jump in blind, as one of my best friends was making connections in the field and was willing to show me the ropes (no pun intended.). I began to work out and train with my, friend, Roger Cox and my (soon to be) mentor, Mark Bryant. Let me tell you, wrestling was a far cry from the gridiron. I had to learn to fall, jump, hit, and take a hit all over again. The one thing I didn't have to learn was how to talk shit. Not to sound crass, but the one thing I have always been gifted at was running my mouth. I could talk trash with the best of them!

I never gave up my job as a security guard at the grocery store, I mean even though I was embarking on a new life as a wrestler, I still had to bring something home to my mom. So, I was still taking classes at Sinclair, training as a wrestler, working, and still managed to have a social life. I met Tammy James at Sinclair. She would later become my wife. It was strange that she didn't really like me, but I knew I would marry this woman.

My life would never be the same. Sometimes every opportunity isn't in your best interest. However, at the time, I wasn't thinking about my best interests or anyone else's I wanted to be famous and as the old folks used to say, "There's more than one way to skin a cat." If I wouldn't be an NFL star, then the ring might be the key to my success. As a former adrenaline junkie, I have to admit that the rush from the crowd wasn't a far cry from the rush of walking through that tunnel on the field. I needed that rush to feel like I was doing something. Being a big guy, there is a certain expectation of you. Either you play football, wrestle, do security, or Sumo wrestle. Otherwise, you are fat for no reason. And wasn't going to wear a diaper in Japan and eat nothing but sushi every day. At least that was my rationale then. I was so desperate to be seen, to be respected. I loved attention, and what better way than to be lit up in a ring tossing people around?

CHAPTER 3

From the Top Rope....

Contrary to popular belief, Pro wrestling isn't all lights and titles. It isn't all fake either. In most cases, the blood you see is real (aided by a little aspirin). The pain at the end of a match is real. The work that is put in to choreograph the moves to keep us from killing ourselves is real. It is a true facet of show business. What you tune into on Monday nights is a carefully choreographed, crafted script, rooted in real life. Sometimes, the storylines come from the headlines or from things over heard, or even real beefs between wrestlers.

Although the matches and events look glamorous, high profile, and all about fun, it's not all big money and big muscles. This is not the business one gets into thinking that you will immediately be the next Stone Cold Steve Austin or Dwayne 'The Rock' Johnson. Although crazy popular and stupid rich, they are the minority. To be honest, you have to be little "touched" to get into this business. I say that because to do this, you have to do it for the love of it! For all the injuries, manipulations, affairs, home sickness (staying in cheap motels, buses and back water towns) that you encounter without getting that big pay check, you have to do it for some other reason. For me, it was love. The love of acting out some aggression, being an athlete, and for at least a few minutes, being the center of attention whoopin' up on some unsuspecting fool who thought he could take me. I still love wrestling, although I am no longer in the ring. I would still be doing it, if my body would allow it, but as age marches on, it tends to use steel toed boots over your body.

I was still taking classes at Sinclair Community College while training and fighting. I was aware that wrestling would most likely not take me to Hollywood and I still liked to eat. I wasn't as in love with the field I chose anymore, but it's where I'd spent so much time studying, so I guess I might as well finish it, right?

I'm certain the term, "affairs" didn't escape your learned eyes. It's true that any time the spotlight shines on a man, opportunists fall out of the woodwork. I will not say that all these women were not genuine fans of "the business" (as wrestling is affectingly known), but they certainly were fans of large men in tights. The term we used for these enterprising women was "Ring Rats". As you are aware, rats are opportunistic and always hungry. These ladies would approach before and after matches and offer us "their particular brand of comfort". Speaking only for myself, I never engaged in a full on affair, however, I did provide a couple young ladies with "their 15 minutes of fame" so to speak. I'm not proud of the things I did in retrospect. However, back then, I didn't bat an eyelash at the proposition of a 'Ring Rat' asking to orally service me after a match. These women had visions of becoming the next "Ms. Elizabeth" (Macho Man Randy Savage's wife). Other's just did it because they were turned on by the brute show of strength and brutality? Who knows? All I was sure of was that I was crazy to say no.

Another aspect of "the business" is the blatant racism. I can truthfully say that I experienced more racism while wrestling than in any other place I had been to in my life. Fortunately, while in the ring, I was spared any of the name calling or racial slurs that I witnessed slung over my cohorts. However, there have been some close calls, and I have to admit that I dialed that number on my own. One match, in particular, stands out. We were performing in a small town in Ohio, named Chillicothe. My tag team partner, Rog and I played the villains in the federation we worked for, IWA. The atmosphere was charged because it was right around the time that OJ Simpson was declared innocent of murder. I have to say that Chillicothe, Ohio is not very diverse in its racial demographics. That is to say, it looks like a cheap chocolate chip cookie. As the announcer was introducing us to the crowd and attempting to do his spiel before every match, I snatched the mic away from him and (going completely off script) proudly proclaimed: "I'm glad OJ got off! Two less white people I need to worry about!" This is what it known as, "Bringing Heat". However, from the reaction of the crowd, I'd say I brought the whole damn forest fire! HaHa! Good times…. I literally watched all the color drain from the announcer and Rog's face! They had NO clue that was going to go rogue like that! To say we were fighting for our lives would not be completely inaccurate. After the match, the promoter met us in the dressing room, and said we would be leaving town immediately. We had to be smuggled out of the venue and leave town QUICK. We never even got to stop at Godfather's Pizza first. I have to say, that if you ever had this delicious pizza (back in the day-at least), you would know what a sacrifice this was!

As my story illustrates, Rog and I were non-conformists. Most promoters didn't even mess with us because they knew full well that it was likely that we wouldn't follow the script. For instance, if the promoter said," Your opponents are supposed to win this one." We made certain that they took the ass beating of a life time before they laid hands on that belt. Yes indeed, we made many a man work hard for a title, there was a time that Rog and I beat up on a couple of guys so badly, that we literally had to pull them on top of us to make them pin us. For the most part, Roger and I didn't even travel from town to city with the other wrestlers. This was due to our reputation of being bad asses. We were more than just tag team partners; he was my BROTHER. We travelled TOGETHER, ate TOGETHER, roomed TOGETHER. Roger Cox was truly the brother I never had. He was my family and I miss him every day. Rest in Heaven, Big Daddy Rog Coxxx.

As I stated before, you don't get into this line of work for money. However, you are aware that you cannot do it forever and it's always nice to know you've left a legacy behind. I bit of immortality for those left behind. Being a wrestler, and being the type of wrestler, I was, I'd kind of started believing my own legend. The lines began to blur between nice Bobo, Momma's boy, Big Teddy Bear and BIG BROTHER ALMIGHTEE, egomaniac, bossy, selfish, asshole. Bottom line, I looked out for me and mine first and screw the world. Whatever benefitted me, I thought it was cool. But I digress... back to the legacy. On several road trips to matches my brother and I fleshed out many ideas to be more than just wrestlers. Finally, Rog and I decided we would create our own, predominantly black wrestling federation the UCW- or Unified Championship Wresting. Whatever racism we dodged in the ring, surely came for us outside the ring, and it was the more devious type. Behind closed doors in whispers and sabotage. Like I said, we were black owned, black, promoted and although all races were welcome to wrestle with us, our main stars were black. We thought it was important for young black boys and girls to see that.

In the beginning, things went pretty smoothly, we were a fledgling company with good wrestlers, run by wrestlers who knew what their employees needed. Unfortunately, as things got busier, and we started to make some noise in the industry, competitors started to notice and that proved to make things very complicated for us. People who before, never gave us a second glance were very interested in what type of insurance we had and was it proper. What kind of licensure did we carry? Silly questions that really had no importance until the fact that we were a black company became known. Before, we had no problem booking venues for fair prices or getting wrestlers to wrestle with and for us. Now, it was like pulling teeth from a dragon. (Grand Dragon?) Even getting paid for our work (and yes, this is work) was becoming an issue. Once our racial identification was widely known, venue rates went up and the pay days went down. The red tape got thick and the bullshit got thicker. Through it all, Rog and I managed to keep UCW afloat from 1995, until health issues, and life drove us to hang up our tights in 2010. We weren't being quitters but sometimes peace of mind trumps proving a point. Through all the drama, and injustices, I have to admit it was probably one of the best times of my life; doing what I loved with one of my favorite people in the world.

CHAPTER 4

The Beautiful People

Wrestling wasn't my only gig during the late 90's and early 2000's. Always, the hustler, I had a 9 to 5 as well. When I wasn't body slamming grown men and throwing them into the turnbuckles, I was still working various security jobs. Over the years I worked at grocery stores, the YWCA (Battered Women's Shelter) and a large public hospital. Being a security guard was okay, as it paid the bills. The only time I ever questioned it was when I was working at Supermarket and stopped a shoplifter. He turned around and shot me. It's not like on television, I felt intense heat, and pain later. I'd been so busy chasing my dreams of fame, first by football, then, by drug dealing, then wrestling; and doing it all, back to back, sometimes burning the candle at both ends. While lying in the ambulance, I clearly heard God ask me, "Do you hear me now?" I wasn't trying to hear or listen; my dreams were far too important for any heart to hearts with God. I knew what God was trying to tell me, "Slow down, son." I didn't want to. These were the best years of my life. If you haven't guessed by now, I craved excitement. However, ignoring God can get you in some deep shit.

I took a security job through Omega Music, Dayton's premiere record store that every kid that grew up I the 80's and 90's knew about.

This job was great because I got to meet rap and R and B legends like TuPac. Yeah, I met TuPac Shakur! He was on tour promoting his album, TUPacolypse. Even though I was working and not hanging out, I still got to briefly converse with him. I found him to be very educated and well spoken. The way he viewed that world and what we needed to do as black people to elevate ourselves from our current state, was inspiring. Speaking with him was a once in a lifetime experience. It also proved to me that the media will lie and concoct a truth that is nothing short of science fiction. Despite the image that the media portrayed TuPac as a thug, a merciless gang member, violent individual. His image beyond the lights was an afro centric, thoughtful man seeking intelligence in a chaotic world. And only carrying weaponry to defend himself against a world designed to hurt him. I learned in this encounter that, what they say about you, doesn't have to be true.

I was also hired to protect TLC through Omega. I got to speak with T-Boz of the group. She was a lovely person to converse with, laid back and apparently the 'cool' part of Crazy, Sexy, Cool. (I couldn't resist the pun). I've had dinner with MC Breed while working for the record company. I never got to do concert duty as, true to form, MC Breed is a true OG and when the promoters didn't have his money right, he and his crew bounced. I learned from this incident, not to sell myself short of my talent, and to not be afraid to walk away from those who do.

While on assignment at the Fly City Music Festival, Dayton's biggest music event, I was hired to bodyguard Destiny's Child – Pre Beyonce' glow up. My only job was keep order while the ladies signed autographs. Now, since I'm sharing behind the curtain type of experiences, I would be remiss if I didn't say a little something about this day. Kelly Rowland was a sweetheart to talk to and she really seemed happy to meet and encounter her young fans. I was able to observe a young Beyonce' encounter her fans as well. They say the maturity brings humility and

I certainly believe it has. I wouldn't say I'm part of the BeyHive, but I respect and enjoy her talent.

My security/ body guarding detail was more than musicians and soon- to- be Divas. I also worked wrestling events. It's amusing, but accurate to think that some wrestling's biggest stars would need protection, but that's what I did. I had the advantage as a body guard for wrestling's superstars because I knew the business. Now to ask me all the wrestlers I worked with, would be met with a blank stare because there were quite a few. I remember having a blast doing these jobs because I was working with peers on another level. There was mutual respect. They didn't look down on me and I didn't want anything from them. We traded stories in between matches and I watched the masters do what they did best.

Body guarding was very educational and taught me more than I thought I needed to know. It showed me that I can be two people. A public me and a private me. Being either one didn't make me fake or inauthentic. I was just preserving a piece of me that needed to stay private because the world doesn't need all of me. The person on the stage, in the lights, is not necessarily who you have to be 24/7. Living like that will kill you. Also, not everyone will appreciate or understand the real you, so wasting your time to make them is not a smart use of your energy or sanity.

CHAPTER 5

Is Enough Ever Enough?

Rubbing elbows with celebrities was a lot of fun and I was "living the dream" wrestling, I still missed the gridiron. My love for football and playing football never waned. So, around 1997, I tried out and joined Dayton's first semi pro football team, The Dayton Steelers. It felt amazing to back on the field doing what I'd always loved since childhood. The workouts were brutal and it'd become painfully apparent that I wasn't 16 anymore, but I didn't care. I was back in shoulder pads again! Unfortunately, being of a certain age anymore has its drawbacks. I was still wrestling and working the 9-5 and now I added football to the mix. My body was feeling the pressure, especially my knees. My doctor took a look at me and lowered the boom on me. He told me that my dream chasing had left me with the joints of a 60-year-old man. God has a way of telling you to slow down. In this case is was a physician telling me that something had to give. So, I made the painful decision to finally put my football dreams to bed.

By now, you've read a few times, God's question, "Do you hear me now?" I guarantee you'll hear it some more as you read on. However, His question was not always accompanied by some type of tragedy. Though God has a way of teaching lessons, he also shows mercy and gives us blessings. However, the two can be combined as well. That's exactly what happened here. Although seemed to the onlooker that I had everything going for me, two promising careers, a wife, friends, and we didn't appear to be struggling at all. But if you followed me on a day to day basis, you would realize how chaotic my life really was. I was wrestling and working, sure, but I was also low-level running drugs. I appeared to be happily married, but I was womanizing. I was living really reckless. God brought me a wakeup call in the form of a beautiful baby girl named, Denise Marie. How was having a daughter such a big wake up call, you ask? People have babies every day. That's true, but Tammy and I believed that children wouldn't be in the cards for us. Tammy suffered from endometriosis, a condition by which the lining of the uterus grows outside the womb as well as inside. It makes conceiving extremely difficult. So, pregnancy was the last thing on our minds when all of a sudden, she suggested that we go to Cassano's (a hometown classic), probably one of her least favorite restaurants for dinner one day. I thought maybe she'd finally come to her senses and recognized the cheesy pie for the glorious symphony of flavors that it truly was. She said she just had a taste for it. Whatever. I get pizza. I fully expected her to eat a couple of pieces and be done with it. But I was shocked that she almost ate the whole thing! When I saw that, I convinced her to take a pregnancy test. She thought I was nuts, but we were both over the moon when it came back positive!! In June 1999, I met my baby girl.

I loved being someone's Daddy. She looked just like me! I loved watching her grow and hit her milestones. I loved that she loved me. I loved being a father! That being said, one would think that all this love would slow me down, make me make wiser choices. No. I was still thinking nothing bad could happen to me. I could be Father of the Year and do everything I was doing before. I suppose it's safe to say that I loved being a dad, but I loved my choices more. God asked if

I heard him. I guess my hearing was selective. I paid attention to and gave credence to what I FELT was important. Little did I know, that my hubris would almost destroy my life and severely alter the lives of those around me.

As long as God was giving what I wanted, or at least was getting away with what I was doing already. Everything was fine. As I sat on that bus, my unsure future getting closer and closer, and the comforts of home getting farther and farther away, I was forced to admit to myself that maybe I deserved what I was going through. However, I wasn't mature enough to stop the childish thinking, admit and repent for my actions. It was much easier to bemoan my circumstance and be angry with God.

CHAPTER 6

It All Falls Down...

Being a security guard was great, but it wasn't paying the bills like I wanted; and wrestling was so much fun, but I wasn't going to Wrestlemania anytime soon. I found an opportunity to be a corrections officer in the Montgomery County penal system. I had law experience from school, and the size that made me desirable candidate for the job. I have to say, I enjoyed the job, although I had adopted an attitude that wasn't winning me any Humanitarian of the Year Awards. My ego had gotten way out of control. The ring was making its way into my real life. The bravado I displayed so proudly for the crowds, was seeping into my everyday demeanor.

I taunted inmates and cracked jokes about their situation. I was judgmental and compassion was a foreign language to me. I had made the habit of telling the individuals locked up away from their families, that "At the end of the day, I'm walking out those doors, and I'm going home to my family." I even went so far as to tell them, "Behind these walls, I am GOD!" I would look the other way when I saw my coworkers involved in sexual activities and other unlawful things. I thought I was untouchable; part of the Good Ol' Boys Club.

Now, as I sat on a prison bus, heading for an uncertain future, and no distractions of my self- proclaimed greatness, I replayed the day my life was set on a collision course for my current predicament. I'd reported to work, as usual, at a drug treatment/corrections facility on the west side of Dayton. Nothing was out of order to my assertation. As I'd stated before, I was 'the untouchable Bobo', believing the persona I'd set for myself in the ring. I was selling and trading drugs (pills mostly) behind the walls of this facility. I honestly cannot explain this obsession that had developed with me trying to be some kind of "boss" or "made man". I was making decent money as a CO, still wrestling and doing periodic security work. But I decided to pick up selling drugs again? My marriage was unstable as well. I was bringing home money, I was somewhat well recognized as a wrestler, had my baby girl that looked like me, I was on top of the world. Tammy should have been too, right? At least that is how I saw it. I'm happy, so everyone else should be too.

There was an inmate on my assignment, who we will just call 'Missy'. She and I had struck up a bit of a friendship, I guess you could call it. She would talk to me about her life and I would talk about mine. I couldn't help but curse myself for being transparent to a prisoner. What the hell was I thinking?! That is a cardinal rule in the world of corrections; never get to close,

Mistake number one. I was also in charge of accompanying her on her job details given our closeness, I never believed I needed to have anyone else with me when I was alone with her. In other words, I trusted her; Mistake number 2. To round things out, I was providing her with pills. Strike three- let's see how I got knocked out.

On one these routine work detail assignments, Missy decided she would reveal what I suspected all along, she wanted me. Admittedly, this was my fault. When a woman, particularly a straight, lonely, inmate is given attention and a window into a man's unhappy marriage, she is bound to develop feelings. I am certainly not Denzel, but I can pass a mirror without cracking it. However, in this situation I could've looked like Quasimodo and I probably would have been a catch. But I digress. She told me in no uncertain terms want she wanted. I was a womanizer, but I wasn't going to put my job and my marriage in the trash on an inmate. I told her this was not going to happen and she took offense. She let me know that either I could give her what she wanted, or else. Or else?? Yeah, right. I was untouchable, what was she going to do? Needless to say, I blew it off. I didn't think that would unfold the way they did.

Missy made her move while we were in the hallway. She grabbed me in a rather, ahem, sensitive spot and tried to have her way. I pulled away and told her that whatever she thought was going to happen, wasn't. The situation had just gotten more serious than I'd ever imagined. I was going to have to write Missy up and hope this monster doesn't grow and bite me in the ass. When I tell you, it was a long damn ride back to the facility, I mean it. "God, what in the fuck just happened here? How am I gonna get my ass outta this?" These questions and the situation buzzed in my brain like an angry hornet. I still believed I could talk my way out of it. I mean, I was a CO and she's an inmate, who would they be more likely to believe? We finally got back and I filled out the appropriate forms, notified the appropriate supervisors and went home. All there was left to do was wait. It was out of my hands, and I was nervous as hell, but I still never expected what was to happen next.

The next day, I went into work as usual. Before I could get started, the Captain called me into his office. He confronted me about the incident with Missy. I gave my account as to what transpired. He listened to me talk, but I couldn't help but look down and notice my work ID and her mugshot sitting on his desk. The preverbal shit was about to hit the fan. After I spoke my Piece, the captain told me what she'd reported that happened to her. Her version of events was vastly different from my version. Her version had me looking like I was the aggressor and that I'd forced her to perform oral sex on me. That I had threatened her. This was so far from the truth that there was nothing I could even agree with! Needless to say, I was sent home. I walked out of the Captain's office and right into a sheriff deputy's face! Seriously? I felt as if I'd just walked into the Twighlight Zone! My outrage was only outweighed by the sheer fear closing in on me. This was real. They believed her and not me. Oh my God.

I was questioned by the deputy, well more like interrogated. I was asked to tell my story again. I told the same story I wrote and relayed to the Captain. The look on the deputy's face kinda pissed me off because it seemed as if he wasn't listening to me. Like he had made up his mind about the situation already. I couldn't let these people know I was scared shitless, which I was. My hubris took over. These white folks weren't going to rattle my cage. I was Big Brother Almightee. I ate intimidation for brunch! I was a CO; that carried some weight, right? Apparently, it didn't. The deputy asked me for a DNA sample. I declined. I believe my words were, "I've seen enough CSI to know better than to fall in this trap." What was I thinking? If I'd just agreed to it, they would have seen she was lying and I wouldn't be shackled to this damn bus, flying down the highway. Anyway, I was released to go home.

When I got home, I was livid! Crying and screaming, cussing and fussing, I called my wife. She was out of town in Detroit visiting family. I told her about my day, what they said I did, what actually happened, I expressed my outrage and disbelief of my treatment. How could they treat me, a fellow law enforcement officer like this? Righteous indignation is the term I would use. Stephen Bobo didn't get treated like this. I had never gotten in trouble before. Tammy treied her best to calm me down. She said, "Let's pray". This comment only infuriated me more. I snapped back at her, "God ain't got nothing to do with this!" "You can save your prayers, God don't care!"

While in my rage, the detective assigned to the case called me. He asked me to meet him back at the facility to talk more. Tammy told me not to go, she warned me that it wasn't a good idea to go before I'd met with a lawyer. However, I didn't think anyone could tell me what to do. This wasn't their life. It was mine and I had to save it by getting out of this. I agreed to meet him the next day. It was a sleepless night.

The next day, I went back to the job. Thinking I would retell my story...again, and that would be the end of it. That isn't quite how it went. I walked in, and immediately I felt like everything went all the way wrong. There was no questioning, no talking. I was arrested., read my rights, the whole nine. Handcuffed and walked out in front of all the inmates and coworkers I'd spent the months before talking to, joking with, looking after. I couldn't believe this was my reality and certainly didn't believe that I would grow accustomed to the feeling of handcuffs on my skin. Once I got out the doors, I thought the humiliation was over. I would sit in the back of the cruiser in somewhat anonymity to go downtown. Nope. I walked right into cameras...reporters and cameras. This was how my family is going to find out why I'm not home yet? On the six o'clock news? Oh God.

Well, that is exactly what happened. My wife, mother, and grandmother watched as I was put into a police car and carted off downtown to the Montgomery County jail. Once there, I was booked, and put into a holding cell with some of the same individuals I used to watch. I'd never felt so alone as I did at that moment. My emotions were in freefall. Humiliation, anger, abandonment, and feeling disillusioned was just a sample of the things roiling in my stomach. I remember watching Monday Night Football through a window in the holding cell. It was the Oakland Raiders versus the Tampa Bay Buccaneers. I was, am, and always will be a Raiders fan; but even seeing my boys play could not lift my spirits. To add to my despair was hearing my grandmother cry as I talked to her on a prison phone. Trying to explain to her what happened when I didn't even understand myself. How did I fall so far? How did everything I'd built and worked for be dashed in a matter of hours? I asked out loud, "God, if you are who you say you are, how could you allow this?" There was silence, deafening silence.

I knew that the holding cells in central booking were far from comfortable. But I never paid attention to the sickening conditions I would be forced to face. I was herded into a cell with about five other individuals to await my fate. I'd sunk so low, that I was lying on a bare concrete floor, three feet away from a toilet and a puddle of piss. Jesus! My life was so wretched that I was no better than to sleep next to at least five other people's waste? When I finally got upstairs, I was put in another cell. To say this was an upgrade in an exaggeration, but not by much. I laid in this glorified phone booth of a cell, trying to sleep with a placemat of a 'mattress' for comfort and trying to stay warm with a threadbare sheet, I began to alternate between crying, praying and demanding answers from God. This irony wasn't wasted on me. I realized the ridiculousness of me being so angry with God, but reaching out to him at the same time. Honestly, as I sat on the bus, I was still angry and in need of His help. Why? Just why? While lying on the bunk trying to grasp my circumstance, God spoke, finally. "This will pass." Seriously? That's it? No, burning bush, angels appearing, clouds talking, cell glowing? Just a clear voice, like someone sitting on my bunk at 2:30 in the morning, "This will pass". Huh. Okay, then.

It didn't "pass" the way I expected it to. I truly believed that it would all go away. Someone would come to my door and say, "Bobo, get out of here. The charges have been dropped." I might have lost my job as a CO, but I would have my life back. It didn't happen like that at all. I was released from the holding cell, but put on house arrest. Being detained at home would have been fine if I was *at home.* Instead I was staying at my mother's house because I couldn't live where my daughter was, given that my charge was of a sexual nature. Even if the supposed "victim" was of age (over 21), it was inconsequential. I also wasn't allowed to work. I was dependent on my mother for everything. For a year, I did nothing but eat and watch television. I put on close to a hundred pounds. However, if you think the massive weight gain was a health risk, it was nothing compared to the risk I was to myself.

Depression invaded my mind. I was defeated. Lied on, disgraced, and looked at as a predator I'd watched my whole not just crumble, but burn in front of me and the world. It wasn't just me being looked at through the microscope either. My distinctive last name made both my daughter (aged 4 at the time) and my wife (working in a predominantly Caucasian environment) targets of the press. How could this happen? How could I do this to them? What is to become of my life now? My mother, and grandmother have seen me do exactly what they worked so hard to avoid. I became another statistic. It was too much to bear. I'm a strong man, a big man, but this was bigger and stronger than me. Maybe I should take my exit and save everyone the trouble of dealing with me. My mother kept a small .25 caliber handgun she kept around for protection. I would protect her and everyone else from me. I took the gun and went into the bathroom. The yellow tile and walls glowed with the afternoon sun as I sat on the toilet crying and cursing myself. Looking down at the ankle monitor strapped on my leg, only fortified my resolve to end this. I put the gun to my head, mentally saying my goodbyes to friends and family, and pulled the trigger...nothing. I couldn't believe it. All logic said I should have been slumped over in the bathroom, dead. Yet, here I was still crying and more depressed than before. I couldn't even kill myself right.

After my failed suicide attempt, I was just a shell of myself. I woke ate, watched tv, ate, looked outside, ate, talked to my daughter/ wife, ate, and slept. Only to wake and do it all again. My lawyer used to try and get me out for proposed meetings, but really to just get me some time outside. I never would let him though. My reasons being twofold.

One, I didn't want to be in public. I didn't want to be seen or see anyone else. Two, I honestly didn't believe I would go to prison, I thought this was the worst of it. My lawyer knew better, but wouldn't tell me. That was why he was trying to give me as much time as possible outside. Wish I'd taken it. Damn.

I got to spend a few weeks at home. It was bittersweet to say the least. On one hand, I got to sleep in my own bed, and spend time with my baby girl, see my wife. But, on the other hand, I was only given this privilege because it was eminent that I was going to do some prison time. I continued to eat my feelings of fear and anger. And instead of enjoying this time with my wife, making love, making the best of things for the fleeting days we had left together, we fought. We fought over big things, little things, stupid things, EVERYTHING. In my prison bus hindsight, it came to me that our feelings of fear and sadness and a lack of proper communication fueled those fights. The fights were cries of uncertainty. Me, for fear of what will happen next and anger for the lie that was doing this to me; and Tammy, for the uncertainty of what really happened? What will happen to our family?

The day of reckoning finally came. I was facing five to fifteen years for something that I never did. I was aware in my heart of hearts; I could have gotten more time for what I was actually doing. Honestly, that would have been a much easier pill to swallow than to be facing the charges I was now. Rape and Sexual battery? I have never been a man to have to 'take it'. Rapists were often the lowest of the low to me, only to be surpassed by people who hurt children and the elderly. Now, I sat in a courtroom being lumped into the same category. A stage three felony, they said because I was in a position of trust and authority. I believe it was because it turned into a high-profile case and it was an election year. They were determined to make an example of me. They had no DNA proof of the action, and letters had been written on my behalf declaring that Missy lied to get paid. These letters disappeared, and so did any chance of me going home. To add insult to injury, Missy "described my penis" as small. To prove their point, I was disrobed and measured for accuracy. They never revealed their conclusion to her claims. I guess it's all subjective as to size. Nevertheless, I was humiliated and shocked that they even felt it was okay to make me endure that.

The lawyer saying, "You are going to go to jail." felt like a punch to the gut. That pain revisited as I sat on that hot bus reminiscing. "What do you mean? I'm going to jail?!", I asked incredulously. Up until that moment, I'd held onto the belief that this would be over soon. "I vividly remembered what God said to me in the wee hours of the morning, "This will pass">It kept me in some sort of suspended dream state. That statement snatched the covers off, a rude awakening to say the least. The following events seemed surreal to say the least.

The judge said, "He can do thirty-six months and then get judicial release. However, if he applies for early release, he will have to do all five years." The DA did not agree with this at all, and a deal was put on the table for four years on a five-year sentence. My lawyer said, "No. Two years." The DA said absolutely not. I sat there, listening while people, who had no idea who I was, or probably would never break bread with me, decide my fate. When all the shouting was done, the judge sentenced me to three years, eligible for judicial release after one. Why would I take the deal? I was innocent of what they said, right? I took the deal to spare my wife and child from the media coverage. My baby girl shouldn't have to bear the (alleged) sins of her father. My wife's job would have had a field day at the watercooler. It was best (I thought) to take the deal, so it would all go away.

I was led out the court, headed to jail. I never got a chance to kiss my Momma, Grandma, child or wife goodbye. The image of me being led away and my wife sliding to the floor in tears is forever etched in my brain. What had I done?

After sentencing, I was rebooked and processed. "Processed' is the best definition that I have for what I went through. A battery of tests was run on me. I was poked and prodded, vaccinated and humiliated; before being put in a cell at the Montgomery County Jail, where I sat for two weeks. Two weeks of sleepless nights, horrible food, and taunting from the CO's I used to be cool with.

The time came for me to ship out to the CRC (Correctional Reception Center). I was given the stereotypical black and white striped gear instead of the county blues I'd gotten accustomed to. My defensive mechanism kicked in and I did the only thing I could think of, crack jokes. Here it was, the moment when I had to leave the city, I called home, to go live incarcerated in a place I'd only heard of. My stress level was at its breaking point. It was either laugh, despite my overwhelming urge to wail. Again, I heard that voice, clear as a bell say, "It's all fun and games. Wait until you get on that bus." And again, He asked, "Can you hear me now?" Dammit, I have no choice, but I really don't want to.

So, there I was, some six foot four, four hundred fifty pounds, with huge tears running down my cheeks asking God, "Why am I fucking going to prison if you love me so goddamn much?" The answer was loud and clear...." BECAUSE YOU DON'T LISTEN." Those words were still ringing in my ears when I was abruptly jolted from my postulation.

CHAPTER 7

Stardate-June 14, 2004

The bus came to a stop; and just like that, I was on another planet. My travelling down memory lane just turned into a nightmare. Immediately, when my foot hit the hot concrete, I was met by THE hardest ass, hateful corrections officer I'd ever seen! His breath reeked of coffee and cigarettes, he was so close up on me, I could almost tell you what brand of coffee he drank. He spat as he yelled for all to hear, "OOOH, we have a celebrity with us! Mr. Pro Wrestler hero! EX CO!! Well, ain't no rings here! And ain't NOBODY gonna have your back when they try to fuck your ass up!" Although I was shackled to five other men, I couldn't help but believe with everything I held dear, that this man had it out for me and only me. As long as I was in "my" city, I had some kind of feeling of security. Right now, the feeling of abandonment was almost unbearable. Fear had embedded itself into the marrow of my bones. I hadn't been here ten minutes, and already I felt as if I'd aged ten years!

The process of being indoctrinated into this society was the most dehumanizing thing I'd ever endured. I was ordered (along the rest of the men I'd arrived with) to strip down, all the way down, to be searched. If you recall, I'd gained quite a bit of weight. I was sitting at a solid four hundred fifty pounds. This fact was a great source of entertainment for the correction officers. They humiliated me by making fun of my size and dimensions. For most of my life, my size had been a source of pride and strength for me. I never felt less than for being the biggest man in the room. That is, until this day. I and the other inmates were herded along like cattle to the prison physician. There, we were subjected to blood tests. I was stuck four times in the most indelicate manner. I was never a fan of needles and this was almost like they were enjoying hurting me; watching the big man wince. After all this, the doctor advised me to lose weight. Seriously, man?! What did you want me to do? Found a prison chapter of Weight Watchers? Losing weight was the last thing on my mind at this point in my life. I mean, really?!

After enduring the laughing and name calling, I was never so glad to be issued my uniform. Who would think that I would find safety and security in a prison uniform? But I did. A size 8X in black and white stripes is quite the sight behold. I looked like bloated zebra. Now if only a giant lion would come and kill me... To add insult to injury, I was issued 'extra security'. I was considered dangerous because of my knowledge as a former CO, and because of my career as a pro wrestler. With every transfer, I was to be shackled hand and feet, accompanied by at least three guards. I loved attention, but damn, I really just wanted to crawl into a hole and disappear.

I was sent to A1 block. I was in protective custody due to my case being high profile and my being considered "dangerous". This meant that I spent 23 hours in my cell. That precious hour that I was out, had to be spent wisely. I could either get a shower or contact family. So, I had the choice of being clean or feeling loved. For the first week and a half, I had no choice but to be clean, because I got no access to call home. This harsh reality was heart wrenching and I couldn't help but think back to my days as a CO and how callous I was to the despair of the inmates I was in charge of. They were missing their families and longed to hear a voice that loved them. I mocked them; what kind of asshole was I? Well, here I was now missing home and the sound of a friendly voice and it being denied me. Karma really is a bitch.

It was summertime, and it was HOT! I mean a disrespectful type of heat! The kind of heat that makes you want to get right with God, because you know you can't handle hell. The heat brought with it bugs. Blood thirsty, creeping crawling bugs. The fact that I was housed on the top tier (or top floor) didn't make it any better. Heat rises, and bugs fly. In order to get a bit of sleep, I had to sleep with a sheet over my head in order to avoid being eaten alive at night. I ask, to this day, was this cruel and unusual punishment? To be honest, though, I was in such a state of despair, that I simply didn't care. Heat stroke, Malaria, West Nile, whatever; I just had given up on life. Life, as I knew it now, was a gaping, inescapable, crater. Everything I'd built that was good was torn apart in a massive mushroom cloud. I felt I had nothing to live for. As a matter of fact, my first night there, I told a guard, "I'm not going to make it." I was promptly put on suicide watch. Contrary to what this sounds like, no one is watching over you with care. I was removed from my cell, and my shoelaces and sheets and confiscated. So now, I was feeling lower than low; wanting to die, and what little shred of comfort I had was taken away. I slept on a bare mattress for forty-eight hours in the psych ward. The only bright spot was that it was cool there. There were no windows, obviously, so air conditioning was installed there.

Though cool, my brain still burned. Thoughts and memories, regrets and anxieties fired through my head like a war. My conscience was tortured, my truth was that I was innocent, but the law's truth, outweighed my own. God's truth said something completely different from everything. I wanted God to believe MY truth, but we both know He doesn't work like that. So here I was at an impasse with God. It almost seems comical to say out loud. Me, at an impasse with The

Almighty. That shows you how high my pride was. As I write this, it occurs to me that God has a way of knocking you down when you get up on your high horse; and I have got the bumps to prove it.

During my "care" in the psych ward, things were even more restricted than in general population, if that was at all possible. Plates and cups were prohibited, even the flatware was paper! You were watched even while you ate. It gave me a new respect for goldfish, because that is how I felt. I felt like every angle, every move, every word I spoke was being scrutinized and evaluated or criticized. If you were paranoid before, it was raised to 'expert level' while in this place. I was in this environment for forty-eight hours, but it felt like a lot longer. I dealt with voices and thoughts darker than anything I ever faced before. While in County lock up and house arrest, my thoughts were (what I thought) the lowest and most desperate that I'd had in my short life. Just when you think you have experienced it all, God brings a new test for you. The darkness that I entered while in this section of the prison was loud and silent at the same time. It was mind boggling. I really thought I'd gone insane because I was hearing voices telling me all kinds of things, lies and truth, hard painful truths. I wanted nothing but peace, but the storm raging in my mind wouldn't let up. Just when I thought it could get no darker, in my mind's peripheral vision, I saw light. This a light I can only describe as God's light. It seemed to say to me, "I'm still here. I never have and never will leave you. But do you hear me now?!" I would like to tell you that this was the moment that everything turned around and I became the person I am today. However, there is so much more of this book.

I was eventually returned to my cell. I'd made the decision to simply 'ride this out'. There was nothing else I could do from where I was. I didn't even care to fight it anymore. I was here and here I would remain. I gave up and sat. While there, I had no money on my books. That means any "extras" such as decent soap, deodorant, familiar food, etc. could not be purchased from the Commissary. Even things as basic as an envelope to write home was considered a luxury. Anyway, all the money I had was still sitting at the County jail, and hadn't transferred to the CRC. The food – I use the term loosely- provided by the facility, was terrible and it wasn't filling, good, or nutritional. So, going hungry was a real consequence if you had no money on the books. However, God showed me that not everyone locked up was heartless. A kind hearted inmate, saw me struggle and offered me a pack of Ramen noodles from his meager stash. I never forgot his gesture. It may have been something small to him, but to me, it was an unexpected mercy in my personal storm. "This will pass" flashed through my mind.

Even in jail, I was expected to work. However, with my status being what it was, I couldn't work much. I was a porter. That basically means "janitor". I cleaned floors, windows and the phones (that I was still yet to use). It wasn't glamorous, but it was a job. I wasn't just rotting in my cell. I also got to shower more than before. (Although the soap provided by the jail was lye soap and it broke me out, bad.) Being allowed to walk around, cleaning, also provided me small joys like watching the Laker's play the Pistons for the Championship. It wasn't a good time, but I know now, that God provided small blessings that meant big things to a man child trying to grow up fast.

I was a "guest" at CRC for roughly two weeks before it was time for me to transfer to what would become my home for almost two years of my life. It wasn't a step up or a step down. I was just going from 'pillar to post'.

CHAPTER 8

I Got the Madison Blues

My day began at four in the morning. The time had come for me to bounce out of CRC and board The Gray Goose again. I had no idea that this day was coming. All I was told, was "Bobo, pack up!" In my mind, I thought this nightmare was over. I believed some miracle had been performed and I was headed home. "This will pass." Yes! I'm outta here! I didn't even care that I'd been skipped for breakfast. I packed my shit in record time. I was leaving this hellhole! Nope. Imagine my disappointment when I realized I was being transferred to yet ANOTHER jail! I was on my way to Madison to serve the rest of my sentence. Damn.

The process began all over again; Stripped and handed a new set of clothing. This new fashion statement was less "Wild Kingdom" and more "Overstuffed Pumpkin". My jumpsuit was a size 7x, and it was too small. I was sitting at four hundred fifty / four hundred sixty pounds. Their solution? They threw a 10x t-shirt at me to protect what little modesty I had left. Oh yeah, I had no underwear on. Yep, that's right; instead of going 'commando', I was 'convicto'. I was herded with the rest of the transfers, shackled, to The Gray Goose, an antiquated, converted school bus, its sole purpose was to transport inmates from one prison to another. I sat in the front of the bus in silence. I was shackled to the floor staring out onto the highway again. I tried to bring up any happy thought to pass the time with less pain, but all I could conjure up was the sight of my wife crying, my mother and grandmother's despair, and my baby girl missing her daddy. And I wept again. Something was different this time. Before, I was in a sort of dream state. I didn't notice smells, or sensations. This time, was like I was hyper-sensitive. I could feel every seam and hem on that damn jumpsuit, I could smell the stale air and body odor on that damn bus. I would've rather smelled the farms that we were passing in the summer heat than what was going on on that bus.

My stomach empty and my heart crushed, I sat pissed off again at God. "I thought you said this shit would pass?" Again, he said, "Can you hear me now?" To be honest, I heard him, but I wasn't listening. I couldn't let go of my own version of the truth. So, I rode, in silence, down 1-70 headed to London, Ohio and Madison Correction Facility.

My only thoughts were fantasies of rogue truckers plowing into this bus and killing us all, but hell, with my luck in suicide attempts, I would have been the only survivor in fourteen car pile-up, missing my right arm or something. And they would've still put my ass in jail. Shit

The heat coming off the road as I got off the bus at Madison is still fresh in my mind. It was hot as hell, but I was thankful to get off that funky ass bus! As I sit thinking about this day, I feel my face curl up again. I looked around at my new surroundings, concrete, chain-link and bars as far as the eye could see. Nothing new here. Permit me to give you an image...Shawshank. Speaking of the movie, the term "fresh fish" was not created for Oscar accolades. It is a real term used to describe new inmates and their possibility to be victimized. Again, my size was a source of amusement to the guards as I was referred to as ""Fresh Moby Dick." Really?

Once again, I was strip searched, santized, and processed. My question was, "What could I have possibly gotten into while chained to a bus?!" As I think about it more, I believe it was yet another attempt to break our human spirit and dehumanize us further. Think about it, your name is removed and replaced with a number, we are reminded that not even our bodies belong to ourselves by being strip searched over and over again. We are herded from place to place chained together like cattle and made to pay for the most basic of comforts. During this continuation of my dehumanization, I was issued what would be my clothing for the next three years, blue scrubs and a white t-shirt. This was to be worn at all times including the white shirt. You would be considered "breaking dress code" and given a ticket if you did not comply. Tickets resulted in any type of restriction being imposed on you as punishment. These restrictions could range from missing a phone call opportunity, to not being able to go to the Commissary for your supplies. Even going to "the hole" was a real consequence for acquiring tickets. The insistence on assimilation always made me flashback to Star Trek and he Borg population. "Resistance is futile." "All must be same". Again, another attempt to take away any individuality. Another purpose of my uniform was to convey to all what my crime was. Blue scrubs were worn only by sex offenders. It was like being branded with a 'Scarlet Letter'. It was an attempt to shame and humiliate us. In a way, it was also a neon sign targeting us for ridicule and perhaps violence on our person. The stories one hears about sex offenders being considered the lowest of the low is not mere legend. It is a harsh and scary truth. To add to my concern about my blue scrubs, was the fact that I was an ex corrections officer. For all the flack I was catching for my size, I can't help but be happy that I was bigger than the average bear.

Man, shit had gotten real. I mean, really real! I was in here with all kinds of people; murderers, sociopaths, everyone. I was locked up with a guy that went by "Little Joe". "Little Joe" was a murderer who cut off a kid's penis and killed him with bug spray. Why, you ask? For his Nintendo system! "This is whole different species of human", I thought. The trippy part about this whole scenario was the fact that he was not a stranger to me, years ago, we were friends! I mean, we played together, laughed together, broke bread! I remember seeing his story on the news and saying to myself, "I'm never going to jail! I don't want to meet up with him, again!" However, here I was looking right at him! The irony of this turn of events wasn't wasted on me by any stretch of the imagination. Here I was, a kid, wanting to do everything right to avoid going to jail; yet here I was, sitting in jail. It still hadn't gotten through to me fully, that I deserved to be here, not for what *they* said I did, but I was certainly no choir boy, and my hands were dirty. I would've rather put on gloves and called them clean than to address my filth.

My new "home" was block "Johnny Bravo", or JB. I carried my 'belongings', which consisted of my state issued wardrobe, a bible, a notebook, a pencil and some paper. Funny part is, I could write a letter, but couldn't send it anywhere, because inmates had to buy their envelopes at Commissary and my money was tied up somewhere between Montgomery County Jail, CRC, and Madison. Hell, it could have been on Gilligan's Island for all I know. I just knew it wasn't where I was. I'd have to wait until Tuesday for my "free" envelope. Just one was allowed, so I could either write my wife or my Momma that week.

Truthfully, I think the state still owes me $25.00! However, I have my freedom, so we will call it even. I'm just saying.

Like I said, there was all manner of people convened here at Madison. However, I was part of a distinct club, The Sex Offenders. Not exactly a rock band, I know. If you had a sex charge of any type, you went to Madison Correctional. Not because of its high-quality rehab program, gourmet meals, and friendly staff, but because that's where the classes were held. Everyone, from the twenty-one-year-old dating a seventeen-year-old, to the predator who raped six little boys in three months was here to partake of the Montecello program. It was a hot class, with A long waiting list. Your chances of release before taking this class, were slim to none. More interestingly, a guy with two life sentences was required to take this class as well. Now, seriously, where was he going? Why did he need to take this class on interpersonal skills? At this point, I believe it was pretty clear to Big Hondo that what he did was probably not socially acceptable; and yet here he sat. It just didn't seem logical. Forgive my cynicism, I'm sure some guys who had life actually wanted to improve themselves, some took the class to eat up time, some took the classes to show compliance and get out of chores. Me? I took the classes because it was required of me. I didn't feel like I needed them. I was no predator. But this was why I was here and this is the game I had to play. It wasn't fair or accurate, but at this point I'd have played tiddlywinks with Leatherface to get out of this hellhole. I sat through these classes, half listening. I wouldn't say it was a complete waste of my time, but I didn't need to know this. I was convicted of a sex crime, true, but I hadn't done what they said. I was a womanizer not a predator. Now, what made me think this was any better than what I was convicted for is beyond my current consciousness. However, that is where my head was then. I was better than these men.

The things you heard in these classes would blow your mind! Some of these men would tell of their crimes with no more emotion than describing what they bought at the grocery store yesterday. One man stands out. During one of the classes, he admitted to raping a young lady who was with her boyfriend. If that wasn't bold enough, he also admitted to raping her boyfriend while she watched! When asked how he felt about his actions, he coldly and calmly stated that he didn't care and couldn't wait until he got out to do it again. I sat there, shocked. Not necessarily that my fellow inmate would do such a thing, but the fact that he was perfectly fine broadcasting it and that he would like to repeat it! To add to my discomfort was the fact that I was lumped into the same category as he. Was I really on the same level as this guy? Did they really believe that I was just as much a danger as this man? The weight of my plight weighed heavier on my mind. "They thought me a monster." Damn.

Classes to "rehabilitate" sex offenders weren't my only opportunities to better myself while at Madison. There were academic classes (I passed), but there was always church. I knew how to 'do' church. I'd been going to some sort of church service my whole life. I should tell you that going to church in jail is a lot more involved than simply waking up early on Sunday morning. You have to sign up for it, a week ahead of time, and hope that you are approved. This process is referred to as sending up a kite. Some guys sent their kites for church service, not because they felt the need to commune with The Almighty, but simply to get out of their cell, or to make themselves look good for parole. I signed up for the former reason. I just wanted out of my cell. This is what is referred to as Jailhouse Religion. And I caught it.

I sat dutifully in the pews, crying and praying, reading the assigned scriptures. To the outward observer, I looked to be truly repenting for my sins. In truth, my tears were so much deeper than, "I'm sorry". My tears were a combination of self-pity, anger, fear, righteous indignation, and just a touch of drama. I was feeling sorry for myself; "poor Bobo, I'm an innocent man convicted and sent away to this lonely place that I clearly didn't belong in." I was angry; "How dare God ignore me when I talk to him?! He said 'This will pass'. Where the hell is he?! When I get my hands on Missy..." The fear conversation was like, "How long until a group of these guys decide to teach me a lesson? Will the CO's single me out? Will Tammy divorce me and take my baby away because of this?" What was left of my pride gave me the righteous indignation. I mean, how dare they think that I needed to take it? Annette Woods didn't raise no predator. I was a CO damnit! They took some drug addicted woman's word over mine! And finally, being a pro-wrestler, I was well versed in the dramatic. If I'm gonna cry in church, I better make it look good. The truth was, despite the hurricane I my mind, I wanted God to talk to me. Tell me why I was going through this. I needed his comfort and security more than ever. I was a child waiting desperately for my parent to come deliver me from this place. But pride is a powerful and destructive thing, so denial seemed a more comfortable place and my growth remained stunted.

After my allotted time for my soul's salvation, I returned to my cell or dorm, as we called them. Calling them "dorms", I guess was supposed to make them seem more like home? Was this term supposed to make me feel like I had a choice in my living arrangements? "A rose by any other name is still the same." Or in this case, a jail is a jail is a jail. My sleeping arrangements were as one would expect, my size had me on the bottom bunk. Contrary to popular belief, this was not a preferred place to be. My head was right by the toilet bowl. You read that right, the toilet bowl was less than three feet from my head. To this day, the smell of toilet bowl cleaner turns my stomach and I get an instant headache. Besides the pungent smell of fake mint and flowers (?), there was also the matter of your hard -fought sleep being interrupted by your bunkie's need to relieve themselves in the middle of the night. Heaven forbid there be a case of Montezuma's revenge. Hell hath no fury than a intestine scorned. As you might have guessed, there was also the issue of "splash out". I relearned how to build a blanket fort really quick. I would tuck my sheet around the top mattress of the bunk, to make a sort of curtain/canopy setup. It served two purposes; to shield me from smells and bodily fluids and also to keep the insects at bay. Ingenuity in jail is a way of life. From storing your clothing under the mattress to save room and prevent wrinkles, to using a bucket of ice and a fan in (the sorry excuse for) a window to create "air conditioning" on those hot ass days.

For two hours a day, we were permitted to leave our "dorms". During these golden hours of the day, we had to "pick our poison", so to speak. Would I watch television? Daytime TV was the devil; but I watched it. Young and the Restless and the Price is Right still find their way to my television these days. Would I take a shower today? If you couldn't afford your own soap from the commissary, you were treated to skin stripping, caustic smelling lye soap; courtesy of America's favorite game show host, Bob Barker. While inside, I learned that Mr. Barker owns principle stock in companies that provide prisons with stock supplies like, soap, deodorant, and other "state comforts". I guess the price is right. But I digress. The last 'choice' I could spend my two hours doing was talking on the phone. The last option here, wasn't one for me because of the tier, or floor I was on, had a particular time for our choices was in the morning. In the morning, my wife and mother were at work. They would not be home to answer the phone. I fully understood that life outside did not stop just because I was locked up. There were still jobs to report to, school to attend, the beat played on; and here I sat. I sat in a cell, wishing this nightmare would end. I was so angry with God. I demanded to know why he was putting me through this? This knowledge that life continued even in my absence made me feel discarded and forgotten. Did anyone out there care that I was stuck here going crazy? What was my family going through? Was Tammy okay? Who was playing with Denise? Was Grandma and Mom okay? The questions were never-ending and it would be untrue to say that my imagination didn't get the best of me at times. My loneliness was overwhelming. I was surrounded by people and had never felt so alone. I cried myself to sleep almost every night. "Was I that bad of a person?" "God, please tell me why!" The still and sure voice of the Lord said again "Because you don't listen." He'd been asking me for years, "Do you hear me now?" Honestly, I had heard him. In that tiny voice that said "No", that small feeling that said, "you should go home.", that time he said, "take care". Every time, I heard him, but chose not to listen and heed. Was I being punished? I mean, of course I was being punished, I was in jail. But was this some sort of preview of hell for me? Was what I'd been doing that bad? I didn't think so. So, what was the purpose of it all?

Until I could call home, My choices were pretty slim; catch up on all the daytime TV and game shows and sit around smelling like state issued soap and disappointment. I had never been the type to sit around feeling sorry for myself, but that's who I found myself to be. I could not shake the feeling of hopelessness. That was an added factor of my frustration. My mind was in jail, my soul was in jail, my heart was in jail!! There seemed to be no escape. I understood why the inmates I looked after acted the way they did now. They'd given up hope. When you give up hope, your walk is different, your mindset is different and your reserves of resilience are bankrupt. In hindsight, breaking one's spirit is what they call rehabilitation, I suppose. This couldn't be further from the truth. Breaking the spirit only insures that inmates will return to jail time after time, believing that they have nothing or no one to turn to. Once the mind is enslaved, it really doesn't matter where the body is. I wish this was a lesson I was capable of accepting while I was out running wild. Maybe, I could have avoided this whole shit show.

Holidays were always difficult in the joint. As one would imagine, Thanksgiving and Christmas are the main ones people think of being hard. However, my most painful holiday to memory was the Fourth of July. The Fourth of July is supposed to be a time of pure fun. Cookouts, family, friends, fireworks were always the things I looked forward to. Although the meaning of the holiday varies from person to person, depending on your cultural and political views, I focused on the popular party aspect of it. It didn't matter what I thought now, because I was lying in bed, listening to the fireworks' show in the distance. I couldn't even see the spectacle, just flashes of light dulled by the clouds. It even seemed like God didn't want me to see the fireworks. I could even smell the smoke. It hit me like a ton of bricks while I was lying in the dark, listening to and counting the 'booms', that I was locked up in a cell while the rest of the world celebrated independence.

Though the Fourth sucked, Thanksgiving and Christmas in prison were no Norman Rockwell painting either. These are holidays focused around food and family. The food was terrible and we had limited access to it. The kitchen closed early, so your yuletide dinner or harvest feast was likely a bologna sandwich, a piece of fruit, and a juice. Being around family wasn't likely to happen either. If the holiday didn't fall on the allotted visiting days, then it was holidays with "the homies". I guess another rough holiday for me was New Year's. A night that meant parties and new beginnings; I was looking at the same 4 walls of my dorm, talking to the same men I've been staring at all year. There were no clubs, no church service, nothing but regrets and reflection. I should have been kissing my wife and daughter, toasting with my friends. Instead, I was looking at another year (at least) in this hell hole. Another year of fucked up CO's, collect calls, nasty food, and that damn toilet in my face!

Just when I thought I would go insane, a miracle happened. My first piece of mail from home! My wife and Baby Girl wrote to me! It was like I'd won the lottery. I sat on the bed holding the letter like it was sent directly from heaven. I hadn't even opened it yet, and I felt joy like I'd not felt in quite some time. I remember smelling the envelope for any traces of home. More than anything, I was just so happy that I wasn't forgotten. Unfortunately, I was locked up with guys that only ever heard from their lawyers. Their families had all but written them off, friends deserted them. I knew exactly how they felt, even though I knew I would at least hear from my Momma, not having contact with home, does something to you. Losing connection with the ones you love and left, is the most heartbreaking thing to endure. You are on your own for real. That letter was a lighthouse in the storm.

I found myself wondering about things that were silly to me before. I was concerned about if the flowers were blooming, who was cutting the grass in the neighborhood, did the neighbors cook out last weekend? Since being locked up, inconsequential things meant the world to me. The saying, "You never miss your water until your well runs dry." Took on so much meaning to me. I wondered now if God had removed me from my life, in order for me to get my life back on track.

CHAPTER 9

Truth is Stranger Than Fiction

My roommate got transferred and I was in the dorm alone now. It's funny how all you want is your own space and when you get it, listening to your own thoughts will drive you crazy. I believe that is because you cannot lie to yourself. You are with yourself all day, every day. You can lie to others about who you are, you can even delude yourself as to who you are and what you did, but in the wee hours of the morning, when all is still, it all comes flooding in. This what happened. I was alone now, with no distractions, no conversation, my own thoughts. At least I could cry freely, and cry I did. All I needed was a word from the Man I was the angriest with, God. My conversations, or prayers to him seemed to be met with a wall of silence. I remember my grandmother telling me that God was always listening. Well, if he was listening, why the hell wasn't he answering my questions? I can tell you the definitive answer. Even if God had spoken to me, biblical style; with burning bush, speaking donkeys, and skies talking like Mufasa in the Lion King- I would have still tried to it my own way. My faith was not completely in Him. I was still turning to man, wanting miracles my way. God does not work like Burger King.

One night, I decided to try praying one more time. I was intently listening to the frogs and crickets outside for His voice. All of a sudden, a voice came from inside the jail. A gruff commanding voice from a corrections officer. "Hey! What are you doing on the floor?!" I jumped a bit, but answered, "I'm praying." He shifted his weight from one foot to the other looked at me directly and said, "You should have done more of that before you ended up here." I was pissed at the time of this exchange, but it was clearly God speaking. "Can you hear me now?" I was so caught up with what the world thought and could provide me, that God answered me in the only way I would listen, the gruff voice of a CO. Did I see it that way though? Absolutely not. I was pissed that I couldn't even pray in peace without someone telling me what to do. I got what I was asking for and still didn't recognize it when it was given to me. How many times has this happened to you?

For two weeks, I was solo; then he came, my new "bunkie". I sized him up, a small and meek-looking guy. "What could he have possibly assaulted?" I thought to myself. I didn't have to wait long for him to reveal to me what landed him here. There is an unwritten rule in prison; one is NEVER to ask why another inmate is in- especially if it's a sex crime. If it's discovered, then, it is what it is. But you just don't go running off at the gums telling anybody what you did! Anyway, old dude just plopped his ass on his bunk and starts to tell all. Did I look like Oprah? The way he came all out with it was like he was describing how to clean a carburetor or something. It went something like this,

"I got locked up for raping a four year old."

Me: stunned silence

"They gave me 75 years, but I don't think I really deserved that much time. I didn't really rape her. I just licked her down there."

I could not believe what I was hearing! This man, 135 pounds soaking wet, just told me, a hulking 450 pound, 6'4" pro wrestler with a child roughly the same age, that he didn't "really" rape a little girl. If I was searching for God, I gotta tell you, that he was in that cell, keeping me from finding a way to stuff the man through the tiny window to fall to his death. I wondered WHY he decided to tell me of his crimes. What in his obviously warped mind made it okay to tell me all of this? He wanted my protection. He obviously knew what he'd done was wrong regardless of his act of perceived innocence. He knew the men in this place would hurt him or worse. I was one of the biggest people he'd seen in a while and I guess his angle was to get me on his side to protect his backside. I thought about his request, I might not hurt him (today), but I hurried up and took the pictures of my daughter off every wall. I know that if I'd seen him linger at one picture of my baby, I would have stomped a mudhole in this man.

While I was still considering being this guy's 'protector' or just letting the other guys find out what he'd done and do what they felt, I was told by the higher ups, that "Chester the Molester" was on suicide watch, and now it was my job to keep him alive. So, not only was I supposed to protect him from the other inmates, but now I had to protect him from himself?! This seemed so absurd to me. As a young man, I hated bullies and always protected those that couldn't protect themselves. Even as recent as the past couple of years, I was an asshole, yes, but never a bully. And now, I am in charge of keeping a pedophile alive; a man who made it his business to victimize children?! Was this a test?

As I spent more time with "Chester", he and I talked more. Much to my surprise (and alarm) he became human. What the media said he was and what his charge was, became immaterial to the man inside the cell on the top bunk. "Chester" had a family. I speak in past tense, because his wife had left him and filed for divorce. His children wanted nothing more to do with him. He'd lost his whole family because of his actions. He hurt a lot by this fact. Not only was his freedom gone, but there wasn't a single soul on the outside that gave a damn about him and he knew it. I also discovered that he was functionally illiterate and a school dropout. Imagine not being able to read what is going on in your world. He couldn't even read the charges against him. He had no idea what his wife put in the divorce papers. His life was at the mercy of others even outside of jail! I couldn't stand it. I had to do something to help him. Illiteracy is a jail sentence that dogs you no matter where you are, because your mind is locked up. He and I teamed up to free his mind. I helped him become literate and later he took the test, and received his GED! This had to be the strangest friendship I ever had, I was in jail with charges that never happened with an adult and he was locked up for something he freely admitted doing. I abhorred what he did to a little girl, but I didn't judge him. I still felt the need to help him. This is a prime example of God's love for us. (I was by no stretch of the imagination anywhere close to the Almighty.) God sees the loathful things we do, and still provides blessings for us daily. In my "spiritual ADHD", I never saw this, but I felt it. God was working on me and through me, and I was believing it was all me.

I started reading the bible in earnest. For all the books of the bible available to me, I kept going back, over and over, to Romans. I read Romans so many times. One scripture, stood out; Romans 8:31; "What, then, shall we say in response to this? If God is for us, who can be against us?" (NIV) This verse brought me comfort in some way. For all my trials, lies, and obstacles in my life, as long as I kept God on my side, I would survive. Right now, that is all I wanted out of life, was to survive. I had no hopes for rehabilitation, improvement, or growth. I just wanted to get out of this sane and alive. My spirit was bruised and bloody, my mind was cloudy and numb I just wanted this nightmare to be over. For all the scripture reading I was doing, and jail church services I was attending, my soul still had a lot of work to do. I was still so pissed at the woman who put me here. I'd never wished death on anyone in my life. I'd never even thought that was a part of my character, but I tell you today, with the certainty of change, that I wished death on "MIssy". Painful, horrific, public death. Needless to say, God had his work cut out for me.

After two months in the Joint, my commissary money finally found me. I felt some relief. I could make a few purchases to make my life –as it was- a little more comfortable. The first thing I bought was a tube of Colgate toothpaste for $3.75. No, it wasn't the fancy whitening, sensitive formula, but the basic white peppermint kind, and it was delicious. I also bought supplies for a "break". A break is a meal made in prison to supplement substandard nutritional needs. A basic "break" recipe is as follows:

- ✓ A can of tuna
- ✓ Ramen Noodles
- ✓ Nacho cheese cup
- ✓ Mayo
- ✓ Onion powder
- ✓ Summer sausage
- ✓ Hot pickles

Mix all the above items together, microwave, and spread on a tortilla, or place in a bowl and enjoy(?)

It doesn't shock you to know now, that many, many men leaving prison suffer from high blood pressure and diabetes, does it? Processed foods reign supreme as alternatives to the food served to inmates inside. When the food you are given is inedible or you simply do not get enough of it, these are your choices, overpriced, barely nutritional items for them to assemble into concoctions. Necessity is the mother of invention. If nothing else could be said to our credit, we were certainly resourceful.

Just when I thought I was going to lose it from my isolation in the midst of thousands of fellow inmates, I got my first visit from my mother and wife. The reunion was only half as joyful because my mother couldn't get in due to paperwork issues. My mother had to sit outside in the car, while her baby boy was inside. While happy to see Tammy, it occurred to me that my mother was most likely out in the parking lot sobbing because of my stupid choices landing me in this place. This also educated me on the fact that families serve time alongside their loved ones. Just because Johnny is inmate number 123456, doesn't mean it ends there. His wife, mother, brother and children serve time too. Their time is served in the public eye. They serve their time in dirty looks, lost jobs and opportunities just because of Johnny's choice. To this day, my mother relives the pain of not being able to hold me when she wants. She is always so sad to see me go. She knows I'm out, but she always fears when she will see me again.

When you visit your loved ones, the rules are the same for everyone. One hug, one kiss, is all you are allowed. It didn't matter that she was my wife. It didn't matter we had not seen each other in months, one hug, one kiss that's it. The kiss was a grandma kiss too. Damn. I can't remember what we talked about while she visited. I don't even think I was listening. I was just so glad to see her, that she could have been cussing me out and it would have sounded like angels singing. I do, however, remember the walk back to my dorm after she left. My heart broke all over again. I took a shower and cried the whole time in there. I had to leave my family again. They could go home and I had to return to hell. While in the shower, I heard God's voice loud and clear. "Are you going to learn now?" I had an epiphany right then. I would stop my disobedient ways, I would heed God. My first act of contrition was to cease masturbating. It was one of the few things I could control in here and I felt that it was disrespectful and disobedient to God. I think it's safe to say that this day, my real walk with God had begun. Although small, I sacrificed something for God.

I gave my very first testimony that Sunday in church, October 2004, right there at Madison Correctional. It was a year to the day of me coming there. For the first time, I was coming clean with myself and God. I need to tell you, that it felt good. This, I consider to be my first real steps towards my pursuit of God's heart.

CHAPTER 10

Different Unit, Same Hell

Also, in October, 2004, I was moved across the street to minimum security at Madison. If you think this was some sort of reward or relief, think again. The CO's here were even bigger jerks, with bigger chips on their shoulder than in medium!

I was dressed out (again). I had more damn wardrobe changes than RuPaul in Ohio's penal system! This time, my 'sex offender' blue uniform, or "R.Kellys", was upgraded (?) to a light blue shirt and 'Dickie' type pants. My prison number was printed across my chest this time. I'd never had my number printed on my shirt before. But there it was, #475..... If it hadn't already hit me like a Mack truck that this was really happening, (which it had), it really, really felt like it now. My name was stripped officially for all to see and replaced with a cold number. Before, I could pretend I was still a person and at least could use my name with the other guys. Now, like a nametag, my number was what I would be referred to as before they even knew who I was.

I packed up my belongings, if you could call them that, after all, I (or at least my body) was property of the state and therefore any and everything on my back and in my hand was property of the state. I was not what you could call "excited" for the move, because I wasn't headed home. This was just another phase of my purgatory. I didn't know what to expect across the road. That's where they told me where I was going, so I packed up, and got ready to go. My bunkie, Chester, was the sorriest for me to go. Crying, he knew he was losing, perhaps, his only friend in this place. I don't think he even thought about his safety, but he was losing someone who actually cared what became of him. His family was gone, he was branded the worst of the worst among sex offenders, so not making any friends on the Yard. I saw past all that, saw someone that needed help and found out he was more than what he did. I felt bad, and wondered what would become of him. I told him goodbye and be careful and went on my way.

I arrived at my new residence and hit the wall of CO's and their searches. They went through my things and they threw away every bible, church item and letter I brought with me. I guess on the other side of the road, my Constitutional rights had no meaning. When they threw my bible away, the CO said to me, "You ain't gonna read this anyway." How the hell did he know what I was going to read? Did he know the internal hell I was going through over the months? Of course not, but I guess it didn't matter, I was just a number. When my bible was taken away, and my letters from my mother, grandmother, wife and child were considered trash, I can truly say that I was genuinely afraid for the first time. I was afraid because this action, solidified that my life was NOTHING. They were all too willing to confirm that for me. God and I were finally mending fences and now, it was being tested. There is nothing the enemy hates more than for a child of God to want to come home.

Minimum security was not prepared for my arrival, or anyone else over a size 3X. The weather was changing, and I was going to need a coat. They took 2 smaller coats and split them up the middle to make a bigger one. I couldn't believe this was minimum security. The final step before heading home, was supposed to be better, right? Wrong, apparently. I knew it wasn't supposed to be Hotel California or the Ritz, but I'd never been in such a hostile, disrespectful environment, or seen as much violence as I did in this unit. Being a (former) CO of color, I thought the white officers would give me trouble, not really. It was the other black officers in charge of my care. I mean, damn, did I let you down? Or was it that I brought the spotlight on your own fucked up behavior? Did they need to be extra assholish to me to show supervision that they were, "one of the good ones"?

I stayed in block, JB154. I (once again) had to go through "orientation". The only difference now, was that the head CO was a female; and she was hard core! I guess, if one gives it thought, she had to be; a woman working in a male prison, and in charge? Yeah, you have to know how to hold your own for sure. She wasn't alone there, as her husband was a "yard dog" at the same place. A yard dog is a corrections officer that patrols the grounds of the jail, they sometimes are found riding bikes, driving trucks or golf carts, or even (these days) on Segways. Her husband made it clear that he did not like me. And she made it clear that she did. She made it her point to strip search me, making comments, while slowly walking around me. Instantly, my mind went back to my days of womanizing and the way I must have made those women feel. They must've felt so degraded, like meat, because I know that's how I felt. Was this my payback from my bouncer days, lingering a little too long while frisking or searching a particularly attractive or well-built young lady. All I can say, is full circle, Bobo, full circle. Although I was clearly uncomfortable by the frequent searches and the comments, reporting this, would have caused me more turmoil. Besides, who would I tell- a lawyer? No. Her sergeant? No. Tammy? Oh, HELL NO. If I said anything to anyone of authority, I would be labeled a snitch, and that tag follows you for life (which may end up shorter than you like). If I told Tammy, well, she'd be up the way at Marysville prison for women. So, I stayed quiet and dealt. When everyone else was searched, their bunks were tossed and searched, but mine rarely was. She could care less about anything I had other than what my Momma gave me. After my "search", I was left to redress and even that, I could not do in peace. She would even watch me as I dressed! Telling me to, "Slow down." I mean, seriously?! I felt like I was in some sort of 'casting couch, B-movie'. Was this what my life had become? Eye candy for a bored, over sexed corrections officer? Was this pay back for all my lascivious actions in the past? Were my indiscretions catching up to me? Could be. However, my choices were my choices and if I was paying for them, it was what it was.

As before, I was expected to have a job. Usually, if you were new to minimum, you started off in the kitchen. Kitchen duty was hell. You were up at three in the morning to cook for the warden, sergeants, etc. The food for the head honchos was like what you would find at Bob Evans, IHOP, or any hometown diner; pancakes, bacon, real eggs. Cooking like this and serving it to your captors really drove home what the slaves must've felt like. Cooking delicious food for people that you never got the privilege to even taste. As a matter of fact, there were penalties if you were caught stealing the "good" food. Yeah, even the kitchen people ate what everyone else ate AFTER we served everyone else. Kitchen work equaled to long hours, leftovers, dirty looks from the inmates, and a hot ass environment. This was the true definition of Hell's Kitchen.

I was spared this fate. By some twist of fate (a head CO with a crush perhaps?), my case worker made me a porter. A porter is just another name for janitor. My job was to clean up, take out trash, mop, etc. Anything you saw the school custodian do at any elementary school, is what I did. Being made a porter right away was a big deal. You usually had to work your way to that position. I was relieved and also a little suspicious, what would I be expected to do in return? I just kept my head and my broom down and worked my ass off. Porters were usually snitches who reported to the CO's and sergeants about the happenings in the block when backs were turned. Think about it, who would know more about contraband, illegal phones, and plans than the "invisible" guy emptying the trash cans, mopping the floor in the bathroom, or wiping down the tables? It only occurs to me now, some fifteen years later, that I was chosen to be a porter due the fact that I was an ex CO. The irony there is that I was treated like crap because I was an ex CO. However, they expected some sort of loyalty from me because I was an ex CO. Nah, Bobo don't play that. I never, once went to any CO about anything I heard or saw.

Speaking of seeing and hearing things, one job of the porter was to clean up the blood from the fights that the CO's would set up between inmates. Nicknamed "The Octagon" (a UFC reference), the laundry room became a place where brutal and bloody encounters were arranged and bet on by corrections officers for their entertainment; not much different than Christians in the Roman Colosseum. Men would be set up to battle to the near death. There didn't have to be any beef between the two prisoners, they could even be bunkies or friends. The CO's just wanted to see who would win a fight between the two, and so, to the laundry room they would go. I never saw any inmate get compensation for his bodily sacrifice. I just cleaned up the blood and teeth left behind.

Not every fight I witnessed required my cleaning expertise, some were just natural consequences of being in the Joint. When men are caged for hours at a time, they lose the ability to socialize and interact with people of different beliefs and opinions. Small conflicts can turn into bloody confrontations very quickly. One incident, in particular, started off as a simple moment of horseplay. Someone must've said the wrong thing, moved the wrong way, and it escalated quickly and severely. A sock with a can of tuna inside materialized as a weapon, but no corrections officers did. Unfortunately, one guy got his face rearranged and lost some dental work in the process. The best explanation that was put on paper was that he "slipped on some water, and fell". Really? I couldn't believe what I saw, or the fact that there was no one in authority to break it up. Any other time, the place was crawling with CO's in my ass, watching my every move, but today, nothing. Was there cake in the breakroom or something? I realized with this incident, that it was me against the world and things can change into dangerous situations very quickly, and (with what seems as) no warning. However, there is always a reason.

Every behavior is a symptom of something. In this case I believe that being treated as animals, day in and day out, carries with it some natural consequences. Also, taking a man's humanity, his name, and masculinity, pushes someone to the edge. Not having a voice to be heard will materialize as violence towards those not wearing Kevlar and carrying guns. So, a small incident like knocking over someone's cup or tray will be met with violence, further affecting the other inmates to react in the same manner. Why? The short answer would be that because they were "dissed", or disrespected, someone else has to pay; someone that didn't just rearrange your grill with a can of Jack Mack.

Another method of revenge practice was taking a cup of baby oil, placing it in the microwave and then throwing it on your victim. This was like Napalm! It created third degree burns on its recipient that were a constant reminder of his indiscretion. Sometimes, the violence wasn't bodily. It could be something like pouring water into another inmate's television or radio. That type of retaliation almost made you wish that your ass got kicked. Incidents like this were attacks on a person's peace of mind. After you fought, you could go back to your dorm, and nurse your wounds while watching football or listening to music. When someone ruins that medium, its rough, because a personal TV or radio was a major luxury that was hard (and expensive) to come by. Your family had to send money (at quite the inflated rate) for you to order a television or radio from commissary. Then, one has wait, sometimes as long as three months. For that to be ruined is quite the blow.

After learning how things went in JB block, and kinda being able to relax a bit, knowing how things went here. I learned I was being moved again. Oh, Great. This time, I was moved to MC block. Fortunately, I kept my job as porter. I wasn't sure if this was good news or not. I was either on third shift or passing out laundry detergent to the guys in the laundry room. Why would passing of laundry detergent be such a bad thing, you ask? After all, I just sat in a chair with a twenty-five-pound bucket of powdered detergent, handing out cups of the stuff, right? On the surface, yes. However, as I stated before, small things could cause big problems. The ration of detergent per man was one cup for all their laundry per day. So, if it wasn't bad enough to have to sit in a hot ass laundry mat for eight hours, but I had to deal with at least one argument, smart ass comment, or attitude every half hour. I knew I didn't buy the damn detergent, but I wanted to keep my porter job and not go to hell's kitchen, so if my instructions were one cup, per man, then that's what you got and you better find another way to get them skid marks out your drawls. Maybe that's why they gave me the job, because not too many folks were gonna challenge the four-hundred-pound pro wrestler sitting in the laundry room. I mean, was your ass beating worth a cup of generic state issued laundry detergent?

While here, I got my next working assignment; a step up, so to speak. I became the guy that worked on the washers and dryers in the laundry room. No longer was I just sitting in the heat, I was working in the heat, fixing broken washers and dryers. Hard work indeed, but a step up nonetheless. It meant that I had a trade that I could take outside the walls with me. It also meant that I'd earned some trust from the higher ups to use tools that could be seen as dangerous. So, "yay me?" I tended to question any and everything these days. Things that could have been seen as good news, made me raise an eyebrow. I trusted no one, not even my wife. I wanted to trust God, but I still was still mad about my circumstance and how it went down, to put all my trust in God. The only thing I trusted fully was the man in the mirror, me. That being said, we know how far only trusting myself got me. I still had so much to learn.

As I said, my walk with God was a tightrope, as I saw it. One more slip up, and I was going to be a Muslim or something! Of course, I'd been approached by the brothers by now. It was an idea floating in the back of my mind, but my heart was still hungry, even though I wouldn't admit it. Somehow, I saw this as weak to recognize my need for God. So, in order to "feed" myself I Indulged in "junk food" by being a "Jailhouse Christian". This is the term used for inmates going through the motions of going to church services and bible studies religiously, but not really buying it. Some even taught bible study or, ahem, joined the choir. It was something to do to get out of the dorm and be seen by those in charge of your parole. (My year was almost up, and I could apply for early release soon.)

In addition to church, I was also taking every "self-improvement" class offered, even the ones that didn't apply to me. I took 'Being a Better Father', 'Anger Management', 'Drug Rehab', 'Alcohol Addiction', and "The Montecello Program." The last course was a class strictly for sex offenders. The waiting list for this class was more than a year long. The people in this class with me: two serial rapists (serving life/ no parole), a HUGE muscle-bound guy locked up for raping a woman and beating up her boyfriend and raping him!

The kicker was that he was up for parole and proudly proclaimed in the class that he was looking forward to getting out and doing it all again! Yeah, he said this in front of everyone, the counselor, fellow inmates, corrections officers, who ever heard it. I mean, DAMN, REALLY?! But most everyone there, like myself, were taking these classes to get out and never have to share this roof with these crazy

MF's again! Truthfully, there were some guys locked up with me that were good people who made bad choices for whatever reasons, but some people were there because the world is better place with them locked away. This was a hard lesson I had to learn. The monsters aren't Jason, Freddy, or Leatherface. They are real people who enjoy hurting others and no amount of classes will change them. That being said, no matter what a person's offense was, or the fact that they need to be locked away, they are still human and that fact alone affords humane treatment.

CHAPTER 11

Man Cannot Live by Bread Alone

I always loved the holidays. My favorite part, of course, being all the great food. I absolutely loved being with my family during that time, but the food was a major factor in celebrating. Imagine my misery at not only being away from those that I loved the most, and imagining what my mother and wife were going through trying to explain my absence, but I couldn't even get a decent holiday meal. Not even twice a year?!

Thanksgiving was rough. Instead of waking up to the smell of collard greens, sweet potato pie, and turkey being cooked somewhere in the house, I woke to the smell of that damn toilet bowl cleaner and the sound of inmates starting their day. I couldn't help but wonder what my family was cooking up for this day. Would they save a seat for me? Did my daughter ask about me? That last question about killed me. I couldn't believe that I wouldn't see my baby for the holidays. I wouldn't see her open presents or wipe gravy from her chin. Damn. I got up and started to dress for another day in hell. In the Joint, holidays were just another day to us. One more day without being home. One more day to remember that no one cares about you; well no one that has any control over your life; the judges, CO's, warden, lawyers, or the streets. That's the one thing that united us all, no matter what our offense or sentence, we were considered throw away people and holiday cheer don't pertain to us.

Chow time is the only time anything is different, and for those that only have food to look forward to (no matter how substandard or processed), it sucked. Breakfast consisted of cereal, powdered eggs, and hash browns. Nothing different there. Lunch is when it got depressing. Here is was Thanksgiving and at 0ne thirty PM, my "holiday dinner" was served. The menu went like this, processed turkey, Stuffing that could double as spackle, something that was supposed to be gravy (but I wouldn't bet the farm on it), a piece of bread with butter, a packet of juice and a packet of milk. As you were handed this bounty of Thanksgiving, we were also handed what was to be sustenance for the evening, as the kitchen would close up right after lunch. WE were parceled out a sandwich, bologna or peanut butter and jelly (we prayed for PB&J), a couple of slices of bread, a piece of fruit, and a juice box. I suppose a more mature way of thinking about this would be to be grateful I was even getting food, or even that I was alive to even complain about it. However, my heartache hindered my Hallelujah and my pride stifled my praise.

Necessity is the mother of invention and when you are facing a single slice bologna sandwich on dry bread, one gets very creative. Thank the Lord for Commissary! Inmates have always figured out how to make the best out of a shitty situation. Its either that or go nuts. Many a jailhouse gourmet chef was born, trying to fill his stomach. On today's menu was a break constructed of: beef flavored Ramen Noodles, a can of corned beef, summer sausage (cut up of course), a stolen jalapeño and onion, butter, pepperoni, and block cheese. All the ingredients were microwaved until bubbling and then wrapped into burrito sized tortillas. Now, this was a special occasion type of break. Most of the time, a break is consisted of whatever you could afford to buy or trade for other goods. A common recipe usually included Ramen

Noodles (always the basis for a break), tuna, a nacho cheese cup, mayo, onion powder, hot pickles, and summer sausage. It was always great if you had a buddy in the kitchen, because then, variety could come into play. Those items were usually stolen from the kitchen, and could be expensive.

Breaks were a sort of "prison soul food" a way to bring friends together, celebrating regardless of the situation, and thumbing your nose at the 'establishment'. I remember my birthday in jail. A few guys got together a threw me a party, of course it wasn't your typical birthday jam, but somehow, it made me feel better about being away. My "cake" was eight to ten Honey Buns, iced with peanut butter and decorated with crushed Chips Ahoy cookies. We had a giant break, with all the trimmings, and a beverage affectionately called a "Foxy". A "Foxy" was made of coffee, three cans Mountain Dew, three cans of Sunkist orange, Kool-Aid, and melted Jolly Rancher candies. It was mixed up in a big jug shaken, and served over ice. I'm aware that these concoctions may not tempt one's palate, but as I stated, when food is all you have to retain some semblance of humanity, Ramen Noodles and Honey Buns are porterhouse steak and sweet potato pie. For a little while, there in the common area, I was among friends who shared a common goal, trying to survive and find something that could be confused as happiness, in an environment meant to break us.

It's amazing how we as people disregard small items like a forty-cent pack of noodles or a dollar honey bun becomes a major thing when you have nothing else to look forward to. It was a serious lesson in appreciating what you have when you have it. God has a way of talking to you without talking to you. The Almighty was talking through a megaphone to me through my experiences, lessons, and people. I was finally starting to wake up and listen.

CHAPTER 12

The Yard

I would be remiss if I didn't mention some of the characters charged with my "care". These were the officers that worked in minimum. You would think that these men would be easier on us than the CO's where I came from; wrong. Man, these guys were more domineering and disrespectful than I'd ever encountered before.

Two of the stand out characters that come to mind were Taz and Handyman. These guys were "Yard dogs", guards who patrolled the grounds and recreation yard. Handyman, a name gifted to him by the other inmates because of his disability, was a special kind of asshole. He seemed to make it his sole duty to "keep us in our place". He took joy in being over bearing and flexing his authoritative muscle on us. He was a classic case of the kid who was bullied, turning the tables and becoming the bully now. I can understand that now, but I have to be honest, he pissed me off with his constant smart remarks and overreaction to seemingly small infractions. Taz wasn't much better, but he didn't seem to have the chip on his shoulder that Handyman had. I never really knew why he was deemed "Taz", I guess it really doesn't matter. The CO's got nicknames, I guess because our names were taken, so why should we use their given names? Kind of a tit for tat.

Things were taken so seriously in minimum security. During the Christmas holiday, a fight broke out in the yard and the whole facility was locked down from three in the afternoon, until the next day. The rule there was, "If one person messed up, you all suffer". In addition to the lockdown, we lost our visits. We lost seeing our loved ones during the holidays. We did get visitors though. The "Ninjas", as we called them. They dressed in all black, and when they came in, it wasn't good at all. They were like the special ops unit of corrections officers. And we never knew when they would come in. I guess that recent events made it necessary for them to pay us a little visit.

When the ninjas mobilized so did we. You have never seen so many men scramble to get rid of "illegal" items. Things like "hooch", homemade alcoholic drinks made from sugar and fruit from our meals, shanks- sharpened items, used as knives for protection, unregulated electronic devices, (phones, tv's, radios, etc.- you would be surprised of the things that people could get their hands on inside.), and homemade tattoo guns. Being caught with these items almost guaranteed you a trip to the hole. The hole is a name used for solitary confinement. It is a form of punishment used for those don't follow the rules. The only problem to that theory is that the rules are always changing, depending on who is on shift.

Things weren't always so dismal in prison. We had some moments of fun. Being an ex-football player, who still LOVES the game, imagine my relief to discover that we would be playing flag football. Yes, flag football, non-tackle, no grid iron, football. BUT it was football, and I would take it. It turns out, that flag was serious business. There was even a draft. I played for a short time, but my talents were better used as a coach. I loved coaching football. For a short time, I could forget everything and just enjoy the game. Sometimes, in the darkest of places or situations, you have to find a bright spot somewhere. It's necessary to your mental health. Prison is a warehouse and like things that sit on a shelf, you collect dust and dry rot. Why do that to your soul? I saw guys do whatever they could to hold onto the precious pieces of themselves before the fateful decisions that landed them behind bars. Men wrote poetry or raps, they drew or painted, some simply read and worked to educate themselves. There were all manner of diversions to preserve their (at least mental) freedom. My method of keeping Stephen was sports. Even now, football remains my escape from reality. When I'm stressed and tired of the world at large, I find a sort of comfort in switching on ESPN and switching off my brain. To be completely candid, I would much rather be pounding some unsuspecting man into the ground for the cardinal sin of carrying a ball in the opposite direction, but flag would have to do. We played our games in the Yard, a community recreation area centrally located outside.

The Yard put me in contact with people from all walks of life that I normally wouldn't have put myself in any position to even give a second look to. The Aryan Brotherhood? Oh, Hell no! I certainly had no desire to share air with this group of people. Yet, here I was sharing not just air, but meals with. I only had one run in with an individual in this organization, and I do mean organization. There is more to "the Brotherhood" than just hate talk and swastikas. They have procedure, handbooks, and hierarchies to being an Aryan; and they knew it. They tried to flex their muscle at Madison, but it wasn't too bad. There were far more minorities than whites there, so a threat- not so much. The run in I had was minor, but this man learned that the reasons for me being under extra security because of my background, was well founded. Never had another problem with them again. I guess good news travels fast. Another group I had the, ahem, the pleasure of encountering was the Nation of Islam, by which I almost joined. Remember, I was tired of religion as I knew it, meaning: church, collection plates, and praying to a God that, I thought was not even listening to me. However, there were some things standing in my way of joining up with The Nation, praying five times a day when I was having trouble with two, Bowties- not my thing, and my abiding love for bacon and pork chops. Laugh if you will, ut I can't do it. Seriously though, I couldn't see treating any woman I loved in my life as a second-class citizen and the way it was presented to me, that was expected. Strong black women raised me and, with all due respect to my Grandpa, Bernice Stephens ran that house and I couldn't pretend she didn't. Anyway, at that time, there was too much change I would have to make. Frankly, I believe I'd had enough change for a while- you know with being locked up away from home and all.

Admittedly, I am an adrenaline junkie, always up for a thrill. However, to be fair, I HATE change. I especially don't like change that I don't bring about. Call it a control issue, but I (like most people) cannot handle being out of control of my situation. Which is why prison was a lesson I learned from quickly. I never wanted to return to this life again, and if given the chance, I would do anything and everything to stay out. Little did I know change was, again on the horizon.

CHAPTER 13

Answered Prayers?

Even though the trial was over, and my sentence was being served, I still had contact with my trial lawyer. I have to admit that I was left with a bad taste in my mouth and an abiding distrust for him. It felt like he collected his money and since I was locked up, he had no use for me, or my time anymore. So like many inmates I lived with, I fired my lawyer and hired a new one. His name was Dennis Gump. I felt that if I was to have a chance to get my sentence reduced and get the aforementioned, judicial release, I would have to play the game; and part of that game was race. Don't believe the hype about merit and all that, the legal/penal game is still very racially charged and the sooner I understood that, the better. Mr. Gump was white, but still understood my plight as he reviewed the court papers and police reports before him. He was in disbelief as to what he was seeing. My case had no DNA, no injuries on the "victim", letters proclaiming my innocence (never saw the light of day), and the "victim's" own unreliability. It was a train wreck. He asked me, "Why did you take the deal?!" I explained to him that I took the deal because I was afraid. Afraid for my wife to lose her job, afraid for my daughter to bullied and ostracized, afraid for my mother and grandmother, and lastly, afraid for myself. I was looking at fifteen years. It didn't matter that I knew I didn't do what they said I did, what mattered was that I was a black man, with a reputation as a brute (even if it was only pro wrestling). I just knew that I would be railroaded, so I plead out.

The prosecutor was determined to see me do all three years, even though I was told I could apply for early release now. I was so convinced that he would get his way. I would not see my daughter or Momma for another year. I talked to Mr. Gump only a couple of times while trying to get out on judicial release. He said, "Don't worry about it, I will see you in court." Um, what? Needless to say, I was not optimistic about his cavalier attitude at all. Turns out, that my lawyer knew exactly what he was doing. Amazing what a golf game and some conversation between a judge and a lawyer will do, because after this little outing, the judge agreed to my release. I went back to court, and heard those words come from the judge's mouth. I was on parole, but dammit, I was going home!

I was struck with an overwhelming wave of gratitude. Of course, I was grateful to my lawyer and the judge, but my whole praise went to God. I mean after all of my attitude, my complaining, cursing, crying and pouting, God granted me mercy- again- and sent me home. I truly understood Jonah when he was spat out of the fish. I heard His voice clearly, again. "Now what will you do for me?" I replied, with tears in my eyes, "I will serve you." I was so grateful that I would have done anything for God.

I didn't have the opportunity to call Tammy and tell her I was on my way home. I couldn't get out of there fast enough. As I was preparing to leave, a fight broke out on my floor. I was reminded why I never wanted to return I made a decision to never do anything to risk my freedom again. I cemented that decision by not taking anything that I'd acquired while on the inside with me. I gave away my extra clothes, My TV, food from my locker, etc. Y'all could keep this shit, 'cause I ain't coming back!

I remember going through the county jail one last time for processing. There were a couple young men coming in, on their way to serve time. They asked me, "You getting out?" "Yeah.", I replied. Instead of looking frightened, these young men looked excited to be going. Like they'd just won tickets to Disney! I know I couldn't hide my shock and, honestly, sadness at hearing them tell me excitedly, that they couldn't wait to get their prison number tattooed on them. Really?! The greatest thing these boys had to look forward to was serving time and getting their prison numbers tattooed somewhere on their little bird chests! I wondered what happened so horrendous in their life that a prison number was something to be proud of? I didn't think about it that hard at that moment because I was too happy to head home. My family still had no idea I was out, but I was going home one way or another. Even if I had to walk!

It was February 22nd, 2007 when I stepped out onto the sidewalk outside of the Montgomery County Jail in downtown Dayton, Ohio. It was so cold, but that first sting of arctic, downtown air in my lungs, was the best feeling I'd had in a very long time. This is was what breathing freedom felt like.

I walked from the county jail, to the RTA bus hub about four blocks away. I had no bus fare, but lucky for me, a friend who was in the same place, gave me fare to get home. Thinking about it now, I wonder if he was another 'angel' God put in my path to show me that mercy wasn't weak and bravado wasn't strong. I'd spent so much time trying to prove my strength and manhood, that I'd put myself (and those around me) in some pretty precarious spots. This revelation is one that I wish more young adults, not just men, would give more thought to. So many, are trying to prove their worth to the streets that they end up forgetting their worth to themselves, completely.

I rode the bus to my brother- in-law's home, from there, I called my wife. She had no idea I was out, so when I asked her to come and get me, she was more than happy to do so. My heart filled with so much joy to hold my family again! I couldn't believe how big my daughter had gotten, but she could have been a hundred pounds, and I'd still have held her in my arms, just like the first day. I could kiss my wife for as long as I wanted. I'd fantasized about touching her again for two years. Honestly, though, I was just as charged to know without a doubt that I was going home with her again. Home. Would it be the same? No. As happy as I was to be going home, nothing would be or feel the same again. I just didn't know how much.

We ate a family dinner; she cooked all my favorite things. I talked with my baby girl. She chattered along like a little monkey in a tree, I have NO idea what she was even talking about. I was just too glad to hear her voice and for her to still want to talk to Daddy. That night, in bed, I should have slept like the dead; but I couldn't fall asleep. I'd grown so accustomed to the sounds of incarceration. Men talking, guards talking, movement, buzzers, were all sounds that became my nightly lullaby. The silence was deafening! How could I sleep with all this quiet closing in on me? On top of that, Tammy was used to closing the bedroom door; and I felt trapped as soon as it closed. I would never get to sleep with a closed door. I got up and opened it. All night, or at least it seemed like it, we were opening and closing that door. Adjustment had begun.

CHAPTER 14

"Reality, We Have a Problem."

To say it was great to be home, would be a gross understatement. I had never been so happy to be away from a place in my life! However, adjustment to being home was much harder than I anticipated. I'd only been in jail twenty-two months, but I felt as if I had just entered another planet, where I was the alien. Being out was difficult, because my case was high profile and I felt as if I was getting looked at and judged all over again. Now, to be honest, they may have been looking at me for totally different reasons; I mean, I'm six foot four and over four hundred pounds! Maybe, they just thought I cute, or it may have been they thought they recognized me. It didn't matter. In my mind, I was being judged, so being out of the house was highly stressful to me. I'd also become so conditioned to "count time" and the officers telling us to be in our dorms by 8:30 PM, that if I was out any later than that, I became quite anxious and worried about being in trouble. Logically, I knew that I was "free", but I'd been institutionalized. I remember being out with my family and I kept looking at the clock nervously. Finally, I couldn't take it anymore and said to Tammy, "We gotta go." She looked at me confused, and asked, "Why?" I told her, "It's close to 8:30". See, I was still in fear of being written up and ending up punished. Why was I still concerned about this if I was free? My mind was still locked up, that's why.

Being around my family was no easier, they all knew where I'd been and I constantly wondered what they were thinking about me. I'd lost weight and looked different, I'm sure I acted different as well. I should've been thrilled to be with my family and friends, but again, the anxiety of where I'd been and what I believed I was sucked any joy I'd hoped to have.

One would think that I only wanted to be home with my wife and kid. Not so much. When I was home with Tammy, there was a specter in the midst- the elephant in the room, so to speak. She'd been "advised" by friends and family the whole time I'd been away. She leaned on her friends and family quite a bit while I was gone. I get that. However, most of her friends and family didn't like, nor respect me from the giddy-up. That being said, marital relations were strained at best. Before she would allow me to touch her sexually, she was told to insist I have an AIDS test and show her the results. Which she did. I obliged, but I have to admit that I was very hurt by the request. "Didn't she know me? Why would she even think that I would even?" Suspicion in my own home certainly was not what I expected after months of dreaming about being home in her arms again. This added to the stress of readjustment.

We argued over dumb stuff. For instance, if my daughter made a mess, I would freak out and tell her, "Hey! Clean that up! I'm not going to the hole because you messed up!" I was genuinely afraid of getting punished because the chores hadn't been done properly, even by my six-year-old child. How much trauma can a person absorb in twenty-two months? Apparently, enough to believe a child's actions can get you sent to "the hole". To say I was messed up, would be a sad, sad underestimation of the situation.

Institutionalization is not a myth. It's real and it usually holds hands with PTSD. Men and women emerging from prison are not okay when they are released. They have been thrust from one stressful situation into another; with little to no preparation for a life outside of the walls. I said it before, and will say forever, that prison is another universe all together. Being released is akin to being shot in a rocket, hurtling back to earth. The culture shock is enough to test anyone's fortitude, and mine was certainly tested. Twenty-two months, or twenty-two years, you are changed. The question is, how do you handle it? One has a choice, you can either learn and adapt, or (and this is a choice chosen by too many) go back to destructive behavior and go back. The latter was not an option, but I put a lot of people through some shit while trying to find my place back in society.

While trying to find a "real job", I found one comfort. I resumed my role in the wrestling world, but it wasn't easy. A few of the guys I wrestled with, knew where I was and why I went. I felt their eyes on me when we were backstage. However, no one was crazy enough to step to me about it. Oh, to be clear, I wasn't prepared to fight about it, but my brothers, Kirk and Roger were. I was the biggest of us, but they felt it their duty to protect me. That's true brotherhood. Friendship like that is what keeps you going. These true men cared for my wife and daughter while I was away. I never was concerned about them being in dire straits. Rog and Kirk promised to make sure they were okay, and dammit, that was promise kept. Until the day I die, I will be forever grateful.

I was able to get a job as an electrician when I got out, but it wasn't to last. Though I worked for a private company, he decided that business wasn't good enough to keep an ex-felon on the payroll, and I was let go. This was a huge blow to my ego and my spirit. I really believed that I could start over and provide for my family again. Losing that job made me realize what an uphill climb I faced.

Of course, I had to report this failure to my probation officer. This was almost as embarrassing as the walk of shame I faced upon my arrest. However, not reporting this would result in my probation being possibly revoked, and nothing, NOTHING was going to send me back to that place.

The conversation was strained to say the least. I was so disappointed in myself and the turn of events. He was able to get me another position. I was to report to Economy Linen. This was a facility that laundered the sheets, towels, etc. from the local hotels and facilities. I had to swallow my pride big time and accept the fact that I went from making $15.00 an hour to making minimum wage. I was going to try and support my family on a kid's paycheck?! Wow. This was more than a blow to my ego, but more importantly, it was a blow to my wallet! I'd worked harder than I had ever worked before at Economy. The term "sweat shop" comes to mind. It was so hot in that place, that it didn't matter what the weather was outside. Everywhere you turned, there was steam and heat. I guess, if I was an optimist, I could say the steam was good for my complexion?

Things weren't any better at home either. My wife was having to support the family. This was a lot of stress on her, and I'm sure, my being depressed and angry didn't help either. I was mad that I was not making the money I used to, but it was my own fault that I wasn't. I went to jail on sex and drug charges. I was going to do my level best to never go back. Did that mean I became an angel? Nope. It meant I was going to be more careful this time while I was selling drugs. Yep. I went back to small time dealing. I just couldn't stomach not being able to put my hands on a dollar when I wanted to. So that was that.

CHAPTER 15

"Sit Your Ass Down." Signed, God.

While working at Economy, I had no transportation, so I would regularly borrow my mother's car, a Ford Focus. If anyone recalls what the Focus looked like when it first hit the market, you know it was maybe two square feet larger than one of those Little Tykes cars. I have no idea how I fit into that thing, but I'm pretty sure that Vaseline or Crisco played a part in getting me in it! But I digress.

One afternoon, while running errands, I was speeding and not paying attention to driving, while reaching for something in the car. I hit the overdrive feature in the car and lost control. The car and I jumped the curb, hit a fire plug, and slammed into a tree. The scene was horrific. It only occurs to me now that I was driving a Focus and was doing everything but that; focusing.

When the police and paramedics arrived, they went right to work, looking, for what they assumed would be my body. They looked on the ground, under the car, in the tree, all around the accident scene. This was puzzling to me as I was standing right there! I asked one of the officers, "What are you looking for?" He replied, "The victim." I looked at him for a second, only to realize he was serious. I then replied, "I'm right here." The color drained completely out of his face when he saw I was standing before him almost in perfect condition. My only injury was a burn from the airbag deploying! When the car came to rest, I was able to climb out of the passenger side door. The first responders could not fathom that a man my size, driving a car that size, in an accident that severe, was able to walk away with nothing but a burn on his arm. I recall being called a miracle. All I know was God asking me...again, "Do you hear me now?" I didn't know how to answer Him. I was certainly glad to be alive, but I wasn't sure I WANTED to hear Him. If I stopped and listened, what would He go on to say to me? I wasn't ready to "let go of myself" and follow Him. Most people would have looked at that wreckage and the fact that they lived, and been at church that night. Not me. After I was released from the Emergency Room, all I thought about was going to get something to eat and going home. I wasn't fazed or changed. In a moment that should have been life changing, I went back to business as usual, so to answer God, this time, "No. I don't".

I went back to work, doing laundry at Economy, another day, another dollar. I went back to selling pills on the side. Another day, another five dollars. I can imagine, God was losing patience with me. He gave me chance after chance to slow down and focus on Him; to claim the life He'd always planned for me. I went to church and even baptized again, but my behavior hadn't changed. My focus was the same, Me. My wife was always a religious woman and I'm sure she believed that one day, I would change and become different. Lord knows, she prayed enough for me, lifted me high enough in prayer to reach the summit of Mt. Everest, but I just wasn't ready.

The truth is, that no matter who prays for you to change, or how many services you attend, how many positions, you hold in church (hospitality committee, sick and shut in committee, deacon board, praise and worship team, etc.), if you are not ready to die to yourself and commit fully to giving up your former ways for YOURSELF, then the words of the faithful are only words of hope. Perhaps I didn't believe I needed the help; or more importantly, I didn't believe deep down inside, that I deserved it. When you don't believe that you deserve something, you find a way to sabotage yourself; to insure your defeat. Victory is scary business. It means doing something that you have never done before. That means work. That means being uncomfortable. That means stretching your limits. Honestly, I was lazy. It was easier to be angry, depressed, and go back to an old way of doing things, while claiming to be a new person. One thing is for sure though, when God has placed a purpose on your life, He is going to have the last word, and you may not like how He does it.

I'd always been able to depend on my body for strength. If I had nothing else, I was The Big Man, the Security Guy, The Wrestler. In other words, being Bozilla was my whole identity. Imagine my confusion when not- so – slowly my balance started to fail. I could not get enough rest. I was literally exhausted the moment I woke up in the morning. I thought I could hide it until my supervisor asked me if I'd been drinking because I was staggering on the job. No, I hadn't been drinking, but my balance was shot. I was bouncing of the walls. I sure wish that I'd had the fun people thought I was having because this shit sucked!

I began my journey of seeing numerous doctors, trying to find out what was happening to me. Anyone who has been through this process knows the frustration that comes with being told that it's because you are overweight, it's because you are stressed, it's because, because, because. However, no one can really figure it out and you feel dismissed by the medical community. A community that you a desperate to gain help from. If that isn't bad enough, people and so-called friends of Tammy were in her ear, telling her that I was faking for attention. That I needed to "get off my pity pot". It's one thing to not have support from medical professionals, but to have to defend yourself in your own home is quite another kind of pain. To say my depression deepened would not even touch the surface. I felt like I was in that holding cell again, alone and unjustly charged.

I finally got one doctor to listen to me. I told her my symptoms and what I was going through, and she said," I think you may have MS (Multiple Sclerosis), I am going to order a spinal tap and MRI." A spinal tap? I'd heard terrible stories about those, but I was willing to go through anything to find out and get my life back to normal. Little did I know, that I would be looking at "normal" in the rearview mirror.

The tests came back. Confirmation: I had MS.

CHAPTER 16

I Didn't Sign Up for This!!

MS?! What do you mean? The same thing Richard Pryor had? I'd never done drugs or lived the life he did. He was the only black person I'd ever heard of that had MS, and I saw what it did to him. To say I was freaked out, would be an understatement. What was I supposed to do now? How long did I have before I was relegated to a wheelchair, stripped of the ability to speak or care for myself? My mind went a million miles a minute trying to digest the reality of my diagnosis. However, there was a small sense of relief that I had an answer for what was going on with me; a sense a vindication, as well. All those people that assumed I'd been faking, had to eat crow and would have to apologize to me. Low key, I'm still waiting on those apologies. Part of growing in your wisdom is not holding your breath waiting on apologies, from people who wronged you. It is best to move on with your life, and breathe as deep as you were before, because if you don't you will surely die of asphyxia. That being said, I wasn't there yet. My wisdom was still too young.

After I'd accepted my diagnosis, I got mad, really mad. I was not angry, I was not frustrated, I WAS MAD. A rage was building in me like I hadn't felt since I was accused of sexual battery on a woman I never even WANTED to touch! I started to feel myself sliding into what I call, "my dark place". I recognized what it was, and I was more than willing to slide into it whole heartedly. My wrath was based in the statement, "Why me?". I missed my opportunity to play pro ball- from a knee injury, I never made it to the WWE, I got locked up unjustly (so I believed), I lost my beloved Grandmother (2009), and now, this?! "God, didn't I go to church like I was supposed to, even when I was locked up?" "I even got baptized and became a deacon!" "I have never laid a hand on my wife or child." "Dammit, I'm a good guy. Why are you doing all of these things to me?" In my mind, I figured I'd been handed a death sentence. Even if I were to end up in a wheelchair, I figured I was better off dead. If I could not depend on my strength, who was I? My whole life, I was the big strong, intimidating figure. Everything I was ever proud of, was due to my strength and health. To find out I was slowly going to be robbed of this, was more than I could bear. For the third time in my life, I considered suicide. I would be damned if someone would change my diapers or feed me like an infant. My pride was already suffering for having my wife have to support the whole family when everything I'd been taught said that that should be *my* job!

I dutifully went to doctor's appointments to learn what my options were. I took my medicines and listened to what the experts said, but not one doctor suggested psychological help. No one asked me how I was coping, but to be honest, even if they had, I would have probably donned my Muy Macho Mask and said, "I'm fine.", when inside, the darkness was spreading like spilled ink, staining my brain. I felt that wasn't allowed to be vulnerable and admit that I needed to talk to someone. Now, you might ask, "Who wouldn't allow you?". The short answer is myself, because I would be admitting defeat. The longer answer is that in the African American world, the one I was raised in, black folk, especially men (especially men in the church), do not go to seek psychologic help. If you have a problem, your faith must not be strong enough, and you should pray harder, go to church more, but never speak out on your depression and never, ever reach out for help. So, there I was.

I had to do something, so I became an activist. I did a series of YouTube videos chronicling my daily or weekly experiences. I did MS walks and went to meetings. I did anything I could to aid the cause. But really, it was distraction. If I was helping people cope with their MS, I was still strong, I was still that guy (in one form or another), but I still trying to help myself. I have to admit, however, that my connections through the MS groups put me into contact with wonderful people, some of which I still talk to. I met my "bestie" Jan, who was an MS Warrior and Oakland Raiders fan (the latter making her automatically awesome). I also learned that there was serious lack of MS support in the minority community. So, I made this my battle cry, my platform. I was going to champion for minorities, especially black people facing the uncertainty of Multiple Sclerosis. For a little bit. I could put a band-aid on the gaping wound in my psyche.

I would have to say, the loss of independence was the hardest thing to deal with. I'd always been someone who was on the go, but with the loss of feeling in my legs and feet, my driver's license was taken away. I was grounded. Being grounded never sat well with me, so I had to find a way to get out of the house! I would catch the local transit bus for disabled people and go anywhere and everywhere I could think of. Mostly, I hung out downtown, watching people go to and from work, and wishing I was one of them. I couldn't work anymore because I couldn't depend on my legs to hold me and a felony doesn't exactly allow one to work as a receptionist. I felt terrible. Tammy had to shoulder everything now. I know she was like, "I didn't sign up for this." I couldn't blame her, neither did I. Denise liked seeing Daddy every day, but Daddy didn't appreciate being seen every day.

To add insult to injury, trying to get social security benefits was proving to be more difficult than I imagined. Turns out that, back then, having an MS diagnosis, proven or not, was not a sure shot of getting benefits. I was denied seven times, with letters from three different doctors. I finally got approved, and as hard as I fought, I was "awarded" $750.00 a month. It was better than nothing.

Over time, things at home didn't improve. I thought things would get better, what with me getting a true diagnosis and finally being approved for disability benefits to relieve my wife's burden a little. I couldn't understand why the fights continued. I certainly didn't enjoy fighting about every little thing, but we did. Maybe it was because I hadn't really dealt with my trauma. I didn't want to appear weak. However, being confrontational about everything, certainly wasn't making anything better for me either. I don't know what Tammy was going through, because she wasn't talking either. The silence was screaming, but no one was listening.

CHAPTER 17

The Reckoning

Finally, the discord became too much and Tammy transferred to an office in North Carolina and took our daughter there. Denise was in her sophomore year in high school. I thought I would see her prom and everything at home, but I guess not. Being who I am, I acted as if it made me no difference that my wife was leaving me. Inside my head, though? Oh, I was losing it! Tammy was supposed to be my soulmate. She was supposed to ride with me through it all. We'd been through some of the roughest years that would destroy most couples. While I was inside, I fully expected to be served divorce papers. That didn't happen. I truly thought we were stronger than this. I guess, once again, I was wrong. I came home one day, to an empty, quiet house, no longer a home. I sat on the couch left behind, and cried. Again, my family was broken, and I was left alone.

I lived my life as a bachelor. I would catch public transportation, (my license was taken from me, due to the MS), and go downtown, watch the people, eat a meal, and return home. I watched television, and continued to do my MS and Oakland Raider groups. However, in those quiet moments, alone with no distractions, I had time to think. How is it that I keep ending up with the short end of the stick? Why did it seem that I was there for everyone else, but when it came to vice versa, I stood alone? You know what? I wasn't. I was never alone. I chose to believe I was alone because it was easier to be angry and blame the world for my choices, my words, my attitude. God looked at me, at times, and I just knew he was done with me. How else would he leave me his position?

I marinated on this as I continued my daily life. Get up, mill around the city, shoot the breeze with the people on my journeys. The same people, in the same place every day. Nothing ever changed except when I would fly down to North Carolina for a couple of days to see my daughter. Then I would fly home, and do the same thing every day, washing my clothes in the sink and hanging them to dry, now as you well know by now, I was a big dude. Hanging a 6x up to dry is more than a notion!

I missed my family. Even though we got on each other's nerves to the utmost, I wanted to be with them. I didn't want my daughter to be in single parent home. I lived like that and I never wanted her to feel like I abandoned her. So, when, on a trip to North Carolina, Tammy broke down and said she missed me and wanted me to move there, I didn't hesitate. My friends and family? They had all my reservations for me. They warned me not to go. I couldn't understand for the life of me, why they didn't want me to go back. I thought it was because they would miss me or they were" hating". Anyway, I packed my bags and was Carolina bound.

CHAPTER 18

New Home, Same Stuff, New Me

Living in North Carolina, was great at first. I had my family together again. I still had my football and MS activities, since I did them online, mostly. The difference was, that I was stuck in the house most of the day, because my new home was away from public transit and money was not in the budget for a cab every day. Thank God for my dog, Sprinkle and cable television, or else I would've gone crazy. I went to church religiously mostly because I wanted out of the house. I was prison again, sending out a kite to get out of my cell. I came to genuinely love my church family, though. I wasn't exactly your stereotypical Deacon, but yet, I was embraced for who I was.

Outside of church services, I found myself slipping into my old way of thinking again, angry and depressed. I had friends that kept me from going completely down the Rabbit Hole. Jan and Christi became my life lines to reality. These two unlikely angels made me laugh when I wanted to do anything but. Kirk, always my rock, kept me grounded. My Raiders groups on social media and television were my major ways of distraction.

However, I couldn't help the feeling that I should be doing more with my life. I mean, I had the time. What pressing business did I have going on? I didn't start on an epic journey to find my purpose in life. God has a way of bringing you to what he wants you to do in His name. I have always been an avid news watcher, since I was a child sitting with my grandparents. I would see things happen on television and I didn't understand what it was all about. As an adult, though, the news and its happenings took on a whole new meaning and social media's viral videos opened up a world I'd never seen before. I have to tell you, what I saw made me sick. I saw things as a corrections officer and prisoner that weren't right. I'd heard stories from fellow inmates about their experiences, and it never really sunk as to how terrible things had gotten. Then I started to see with a new set of eyes about the plight of men and women behind bars. I saw the injustice that my brothers and sisters suffered for just being the wrong color or tax bracket. Someone had to tell the world about these atrocities! I mean, why was this alright? And just like that, my purpose was born. I would be an advocate. I would raise my voice against those running a system determined to silence the little guy.

I started small. I just shared videos on social media with messages about how messed up it was. I would make little live videos expressing my frustration with the system. I have always been a bit of a conspiracy theorist; militant against the system meant to make us puppets. I raised my fist when the National Anthem played. However, I never dreamed that I would turn this mission into my life's work.

I began fighting for prisoner's rights. Being a former inmate, this was a cause near and dear to my heart. I firmly believe that treating human beings like animals, without basic needs met, does not "rehabilitate" it simply makes a person bitter and it furthers the feelings on anxiety, anger and resentment. It turns out a human being who is a mere shadow of him or herself. This person, upon release, would be unprepared for life on the outside. To be honest, they barely could survive on the inside as fully functioning adult. Being stripped of your freedom is traumatic enough, regardless of offense, but to not only be locked up, but to suffer shoddy basic healthcare, food not good enough to be given to farm creatures, indignities and humiliation on a daily basis, is inhumane. This became my first adventure into the advocacy issues of the prisoner population. This gave me purpose. I felt like I was finally doing something worthwhile.

I started to reach out to incarcerated individuals and their families. I wanted to hear their stories. People always focus on the person in the jail, but they rarely stop to consider the families left behind. The families serve time too. Wives have to answer questions at family functions or work. Mothers have to endure whispers about what they must've done wrong and kids have to deal with mean comments and being ostracized and bullied because of their family member who made a bad choice. So, to say the person locked up suffers alone is a vast miscalculation of the situation. These are subjects I took on full force, cheered on my small but fierce support system.

Being a man of minority status, I also felt need to stand up for my fellow people who couldn't pass the" paper bag test". Stories like Trayvon Martin, Sandra Bland, Philandro Castle spurred my resolve to see justice and fair treatment of people who had the misfortune to encounter overzealous police officers. This became a secondary cause for me, although I never saw it as an issue less important, it has just become another talking point I needed to touch upon.

Around this time, I connected with an old friend. As the story es, she was scrolling through Facebook, and saw I comment I made on a mutual friend's post and she wondered if I was who she thought I was and after some trolling on the internet, she made a request to be "friends". Honestly, I didn't recognize her at first (she looked quite different from the 16year old hanging out in the rec room). But there she was little Dani.

She wasn't so "little" anymore. I almost didn't even recognize her! Man, whatever she was doing must've been right, because this girl was FINE! We reconnected and talked almost every day. I found out she shared my passion for speaking up for those who couldn't do it for themselves. We talked about our lives while apart. We found out that prior to me moving to North Carolina to try and make my marriage work, she and I were never more than five minutes away from each other. Often crossing paths or common acquaintances, without ever running into each other! Talk about crazy!

She listened to me talk about writing a book about my life; and starting an organization for returning citizens. I told her about my life and the circumstances that led to me being where I was. She never passed judgement on me or pulled back because of who I was or what I was. That taught me that people were not as awful as I'd assumed, and it gave me the push to write this book. To tell people that your past doesn't have to be your future. That God talks and guides even when you won't listen. However, when you don't listen and you ignore his, "Do you hear Me now", he will move in ways to MAKE you listen, to heed.

So many times, God spoke, and due to my unwillingness to submit and my belief that I was more powerful, that I knew more than the force that created me, that I missed the following signs:

- Getting shot and surviving
- 2 failed suicide attempts
- Going to Jail
- A car accident that should have killed me and I walked away
- My beautiful daughter being born against the odds
- Multiple Sclerosis

There were so many other incidents, infinite ones I had no idea about, but yet, I survived. I have not just survived, but I have thrived. Now, this revelation has not been wasted on me. Only now, have I come to the realization that God had a purpose for me. So often, we don't understand that God has a purpose for us. We assume that because it isn't happening right away, or we have not been handed a game plan from "above", we have no purpose. That belief leads us to make choices that are detrimental and contrary to "the plan". I am the prime example of this way of thinking. My choices, were just that, MINE. However, I tended to drag so many people I loved with me. It did a lot of damage. I believe that this damage in the course of trying to do the right thing, is what fuels my kinship with Godzilla. While fighting the monsters trying to destroy humanity, he ends up making a huge mess. Poor Tokyo. The question is, though, had he stayed on the island of monsters, how much trouble would the world be in? I guess we will leave those ponderances to the movie writers.

The point is, that I got several second chances and there were men and women sitting in cells, just wanting one second chance. There were kids in the 'hood' that were looking for just one first chance. This is what fueled my passion for the Prison Watch groups, End the School to Prison Pipeline groups, public speaking and mentoring endeavors; my conviction that everyone deserves a chance to be great. "Life, Liberty, and the Pursuit of Happiness" is a core value of our country. Yet, so many people (usually the 99% not residing in the upper echelons of society) are shunned from this ideal laid by our founding fathers.

Don't get me wrong, the choices that people make hold with them a certain amount of accountability. The first part of that sentence had a critical word in it, "choice". If a person doesn't believe they have any choices, their decisions are flawed. My mission in life is to let incarcerated persons and at-risk youth know that they do have choices. You do not have to join a gang; you do not have to sell drugs. There is another road. The road may not be easy, understood, or even respected, but it's YOUR road. It is your responsibility to make it a good one. No matter how old you are, you have choices; to either be better, or be a statistic. Statistics do not make history, they make data sheets- nameless, replaceable, unremarkable datasheets. Everyone's mother gave them a name. No matter what you think today, you are irreplaceable. Everyone has a remarkable quality; develop it and claim your superpower!

I decided that I would "pass the mic" to the people being silenced; the people with loved ones locked up and told to accept whatever was done to them. I was on both sides of the bars and there are things happening that even I didn't know! All kinds of rights being violated, constitutional and human! I was appalled to learn of the conditions people (yes, they are still people- despite their crime) were being forced to live in. These are conditions that if we saw animals living in, we would be marching and protesting and raising hell from the mountaintops. However, because it is a person behind bars, it's okay. No. Regardless of what we think of these people, we need to keep in mind that they are humans who made some mistakes (and sometimes the mistake was simply being in the wrong place at the wrong time), and no one should cease to be treated with human decency. This is the cause I champion. I took my former moniker, Bozilla and decided to give him a new mission. From now on, Bozilla would use his size and power to fuel a movement.

CHAPTER 19

Where Do We Go From Here?

So, here we are. End the School to Prison Pipeline encourages kids to think about their choices, realize that they do have choices and to use the grit they have to make positive choices, even if it means going against the grain. The only way to clog up this pipeline is to keep kids from being distracted from their own innate greatness, and keeping them aware of their worth. My staff- headed, by strong, determined women like my beloved grandmother and mother keep things in order and help me stay grounded. Thank you, ladies.

Bozilla Blogtalk radio gives a voice to those already locked up. I "pass the mic" to them to let the public know what is happening. To use the power of media for good. Just because a man woman or child is locked up, doesn't mean they cease to have worth or intelligence, or talent. My shows bring that to light. It gives voice to mothers, wives, and loved one of incarcerated individuals serving time alongside their family.

What about Stephen Bobo? I am still growing and I am not where I want to be, but I'm so grateful to God for not being where I was. I still fail, fall, and stumble my way through life (literally and figuratively). However, now, I know I have choices and I hold myself accountable for the all. My marriage didn't make it through the changes. But that's okay. Growth sometimes means leaving the old behind. I still have mad love for Tammy. She was a is still a phenomenal lady and she has greatness destined for her. I wish her nothing but the best and am eternally grateful to her for the years we had. I've moved on with the lessons I learned and plan to be a better man for it.

My daughter, Denise Marie is 20 now, and talented and brilliant. I have never had any doubt that she loved me, even at my worst. I have always loved her, from the confines of her mother's womb, through the bars of a jail cell, and now from across the country. She is my air and my reason for what I do. I want to show her that her "old man" can make a difference and so can she.

I was Convicted as a criminal, but before that I was Convicted an immature hard headed, selfish man. God had to sit me down in a jail cell, then within my own body to make me realize His plan. Now, I get to walk in the Redemption and relief of knowing my worth, knowing His love, and spreading the Gospel through my actions to those still struggling. At the end of the day, I just want to know that someone was able to see my example and change their life. Whether it be the good example and followed it, or my mistakes, and took that they didn't want the same thing to happen Either way, if one person changes their life for the better, I have done my job and Bozilla may rest easy in the kelp.

ABOUT THE AUTHORS

STEPHEN BOBO is a motivational speaker, activist and author based out of Columbus, Ohio. Stephen was born in Columbus, Ohio and raised in Dayton, Ohio and Springfield, Ohio.

He is the proud Father of Denise Bobo, son of Annette Woods and Grady Bobo and card carrying member of The Raider Nation.

DANIELLE ANDREWS is a Dayton born writer, visual artist and activist for Autism rights. She is a graduate of both Sinclair Community College and Wright State University. Danielle is the proud mother of Tera, 25 and Gryffin, 7.

Ms. Andrews enjoys a 20-year career teaching and aiding those with special needs. She takes great pride in her activism for those with Autism. A passion awakened when her son was diagnosed in 2016. She is currently working to get her MA in art therapy with teens and adolescents.

As a visual artist, Danielle loves to use materials that others would throw away. Her art tells stories of struggle, reflection and rebirth.

Becoming a writer was purely coincidental as she and Mr. Bobo sat talking about dreams one night. He spoke of his dream to write a book about his experiences, and she said "Then let's do it." Sitting in a sports bar in Kentucky, the two sat down, grabbed a notebook, and the story began. Her writing style is conversational and colorful. She enjoys writing in the voice of the subject for authenticity.

Printed in the United States
By Bookmasters